Praise For
The Retailer's Complete Book of Selling Games and Contests

"This is one book that doesn't collect dust in our stores. We use it to spice things up and build a competitive spirit. I particularly like the contests designed to teach our salespeople how to sell merchandise they wouldn't normally sell. A great sales tool for any retailer."

—Russ Diamond,
Snyder Diamond

"I can't imagine a successful retailer not wanting this collection of retail games and contests in each of their stores. A great way to motivate your staff and brew up sales when traffic is slow. A real money-maker!"

—Howard Fineman,
Ashley Furniture HomeStore

"*The Retailer's Complete Book of Selling Games and Contests* really made a huge impact with our team. We've noticed increased competitiveness, excitement, and an improved quality of sales during our contests."

—Dr. Stephen Fahringer,
Good Feet Stores

THE **RETAILER'S**
COMPLETE BOOK OF
SELLING
GAMES AND **CONTESTS**

THE **RETAILER'S** COMPLETE BOOK OF **SELLING** GAMES AND **CONTESTS**

OVER **100 SELLING GAMES** FOR INCREASING ON-THE-FLOOR PERFORMANCE

HARRY J. FRIEDMAN

WILEY

John Wiley & Sons, Inc.

Published by John Wiley & Sons, Inc., Hoboken, New Jersey.
Published simultaneously in Canada.

For general information on our other products and services or for technical support, please contact our Customer Care Department within the United States at (800) 762-2974, outside the United States at (317) 572-3993 or fax (317) 572-4002.

Wiley publishes in a variety of print and electronic formats and by print-on-demand. Some material included with standard print versions of this book may not be included in e-books or in print-on-demand. If this book refers to media such as a CD or DVD that is not included in the version you purchased, you may download this material at http://booksupport.wiley.com. For more information about Wiley products, visit www.wiley.com.

ISBN: 978-1-118-15341-3 (paper)
ISBN: 978-1-118-21643-9 (ebk)
ISBN: 978-1-118-21646-0 (ebk)
ISBN: 978-1-118-21647-7 (ebk)

Printed in the United States of America
10 9 8 7 6 5 4 3 2 1

Over the years, there have been many retailers who have shared with me the most successful games and contests they have run. Fortunately, there are those who share my enthusiasm for fun and profit.

Because of the way this book came together, it was difficult to attribute the original games to specific people. Sometimes, several different people came up with the same idea for a game. To that end, if you think you invented a game or contest contained in the book, be my guest and take full credit—you deserve it.

There are some very important people to acknowledge for their contributions to the book. First is Sandra Lamplugh, who got the whole thing started, suffering through hours of audio tapes I recorded on the subject of games. Next is Barbara Sosa, who continued the process and tightened the concept. And finally, there's Liz Cichowski, who may be the fastest and best writer in town—she just gets it done.

A special thank-you to Gary Solomon and Susan Siegel for the artwork, and to the great staff at The Friedman Group for helping in any way they could to get this book out. It was quite a group effort.

THE FRIEDMAN GROUP
Retail Consulting & Training

Delivering sales increases for retailers worldwide since 1980

Call: 800–351–8040 or 310–590–1248

E-mail: Info@TheFriedmanGroup.com • **Website:** www.TheFriedmanGroup.com

5759 Uplander Way, Culver City, CA 90230, USA

United States • Mexico • Central America • Colombia • Ecuador • Argentina • Chile • Brazil • New Zealand • Australia • South Africa • India

Harry J. Friedman

TABLE OF CONTENTS

FUN & GAMES!

*When something
is rewarding,
it gets done.*

It's unrealistic to assume that all retail salespeople show up for work each day excited about selling and contributing to their store's success. Personal observation and experience have shown that for many staff members, the thrill of a new job is gone after only a few months. The newness of the job easily fades into a routine. There's no question about it—selling can be a repetitive process. Selling the same furniture, lamps, or stereo systems, day after day, can get boring. And doing boring things isn't fun or challenging. Boring things don't provide people with the opportunities they need to feel a sense of accomplishment or achievement. Without such opportunities, your salespeople are not likely to become the professionals you want them to be.

The people who work in your store aren't volunteers. They're paid to work and to meet your store's standards. However, if your salespeople see work only as a source of income and never as a source of satisfaction, enjoyment, or fun, then wanting to do their personal best will be ignored. Learning, self-worth, cultivating customers, going that extra mile, and really wanting to excel result from much more than a paycheck. Salespeople don't always go for it without something extra—some kind of incentive. It's your job to find ways to give them incentives and provide them with opportunities to get recognition for a job well done. It's your job to help them find the motivation to reach their full potential.

This book is a motivational tool. It is a compilation of contests and games that are proven to be incredibly motivating! I've seen how contests and games cause people to do extraordinary things. They give people targets to shoot for. They create competitiveness. In my own company, we constantly run contests and games. Why? Because they're fun, they get people more involved, and they work.

The difference can be absolutely amazing! Just by providing some kind of a finish line and a reward, you can change a staff member's entire attitude and behavior on the selling floor. Suddenly, the same person who wasn't motivated enough to show up on time begins to improve his or her selling skills and wants to do more and more—to *go for it*. When there's a game or a contest going on, you'll see how your salespeople will take that one extra shot. Why is that? Because most of us have a natural desire to succeed. Most of us enjoy a challenge. And most of us want to win!

At this point, you might be thinking about skipping ahead to Chapter 5, where you'll find our collection of over 100 retail contests, games, and variations. Since it's a good idea to learn how to use a tool properly before picking it up and working with it, I urge you to first read the four introductory chapters. These chapters will give you the foundation you need to maximize the potential of the contests and games you'll find in Chapter 5.

Contests and games improve performance—it's as simple as that.

Chapter One: "Why Have Games?"
In order to get the most from a game or contest, you need to understand the reason behind it. The only reason you run a game or contest is to improve a sales statistic or selling behavior. A game is valid only when you run it to get a significant return on your investment of time, money, and so on. Chapter 1 explains this in detail.

Chapter Two: "Elements of a Game"
There are 10 elements that you must consider in order to run a successful game or contest, including how to determine rewards or prizes for the winners. This chapter gives you essential information on planning for and controlling each element to your benefit.

Chapter Three: "Selling the Game to Your Staff"
This chapter addresses methods of establishing and demonstrating leadership qualities in your store. That leadership will help you to sell and promote games and contests so that everyone will play.

Chapter Four: "Making Your Case and Establishing a Reward System"
Chapter 4 explains sources for contest money and innovative rewards that you can provide for your salespeople. This chapter also includes a discussion of how to justify games to upper management. After you read this information, you'll be ready to get going with your first game.

Chapter Five: "Fun and Games!"
Here they are. All the selling games and contests are in this chapter and explained in a standard format that makes them easy to use. Let the games begin!

Before you move on to Chapter 1, I'd like to make the point that while we believe strongly in aggressive and bold selling, we also believe that good selling techniques and customer service skills always apply. Professional selling and excellent customer service should be evident regardless of the game, contest, or incentive. So, when you talk to your salespeople about games, remind them:

Always do the right thing for the customer, and provide the best customer service you possibly can.

Retail selling must be fun for both customers and salespeople. Used properly, games and contests will help your salespeople maximize their sales and have a good time doing so. Games and contests are fun. They create a mood that says, "Let's play! Let's enjoy ourselves!" They create an atmosphere that attracts customers and makes them remember your store. It is truly this kind of spirit that we want to create every single day. Have fun with the games and contests in this book, and enjoy the sales increases you'll see as a result!

If you knew of a game that would get your salespeople to do extraordinary things to increase their sales, wouldn't you take a shot at it? I'm betting that you would!

The only reason to run a game or a contest is to improve a sales metric or a selling behavior.

Let's say you discovered that running games or contests all the time would breathe some life into your store, creating an atmosphere in which both your customers and salespeople really enjoyed themselves. Would you begin to run games and contests? Naturally . . . all the time!

I strongly believe in games. There's no question about it—games and contests have a stimulating effect on people. They bring out the fun, the challenging and competitive spirit in all of us. After all, who doesn't want to play and win?

Think about how tremendously involved we become when watching professional basketball, baseball, boxing, or horse racing. Emotionally, we get right out there with the key players, don't we? We want them to measure up to our expectations and prove they can go out there and do it. We want them to win!

And what about the games we participate in, such as bowling, golf, and tennis? People actively involved in these games feel very strongly about the idea of competing and the results of stretching themselves to their own individual limits.

There is an excitement and an enthusiasm that builds as players prepare for "the game." They can't wait to see how they'll do. Both top professionals and amateurs in any field work very hard to reach their personal best. Their object is to be the best they can be: to get a better score than last time—to show progress.

Using games and contests, you can create the same competitive and challenging atmosphere. But that atmosphere isn't the only thing you're looking for.

The improvements in selling behaviors and sales statistics that result from that atmosphere are the real reason that you run games. Your salespeople will constantly find ways to improve their skills and beat their figures for each event.

Games and Contests Improve Statistics

I think we would all agree that salespeople who make their living from commissions, or who are otherwise held accountable for their sales, love the idea of knowing how well they're doing. They want to know how their sales rate in relation to store averages, company averages, their friend Frank's averages, or even to their own personal potential.

Scores and statistics are important. They become benchmarks. They let us know how well we're doing, whether or not we reach our mark, or when we top it. The object of any retail game or contest is to get your salespeople to want to reach a goal—to do better or to meet or beat a sales statistic. That's what makes games very competitive.

So, if you want to improve a statistic—any statistic—run a game or have a contest! When you put that kind of attention on something, spotlighting a part of your business, things happen.

For example, I had a shoe client in the early 1980s that needed to improve the items-per-sale statistic. The average was running at about 1.30 pairs of shoes sold per transaction. In

After you run a contest or game and your store's numbers improve, you should never expect those numbers to go down again.

the shoe business, as with most retail operations, add-on sales are the key to growth and profit. We labored through extensive sales training and many meetings, extolling the virtues of adding on, but the resultant increases were small.

Around that same time, Imelda Marcos, wife of the Philippines' deposed president, was pictured in the papers with a closet full of shoes (about 2,000 pairs). A light bulb went on, and a contest was formed: the Imelda Marcos Cup!

This contest awarded terrific prizes for those individuals who maintained large items-per-sale increases. The Imelda Marcos Cup ran for about a week, and items per sale rose to a company-wide average of 1.75.

Everyone was happy, and a number of prizes were distributed. After a couple of weeks, the average settled at about 1.45 items per sale—0.15 above the original average. Now that the sales staff knew they could sell more items per sale, management was able to expect the staff to maintain a higher level of performance.

Why is this so? In the above case, the staff already proved that items per sale could reach as high as 1.75. Since the object of a game or contest is to beat a statistic—to do better—and items per sale increased to 1.75, that became the new score to beat. Now, each store may not maintain that statistic all the time, but the incremental increase over 1.30 is where all the money is made. That's what's so exciting about contests and games!

Games and Contests Improve and Enhance Selling Behaviors

Improved selling behaviors are directly related to the focus that games and contests place on sales statistics. A behavior is an activity that can be seen, described, or measured. Selling behaviors are how your sales staff sells. All behaviors, including selling behaviors, can be reinforced with positive consequences.

Behaviors may very well be determined by the consequences that follow. Get a prize for doing something special, and you will probably want to do it again.

For example, if running the games and contests in this book becomes a behavior on your part, and you see your store's sales statistics go up, then the likelihood that you'll continue to run more games and contests will increase, right? Of course it will, because the experience was positive and rewarding and what you accomplished was exciting and successful.

When your salespeople start associating desirable events like winning money and prizes with improved selling behaviors, they'll want to keep on improving their selling behaviors. When they associate doing extraordinary things on the selling floor with having fun, they'll want to do those things over and over again.

The Socialization Process
One more benefit of running contests and games, particularly team games, results from the socialization process. The process of being teamed up with others and working toward a common goal encourages cooperation and improved communication. People learn to share ideas and feelings with each other, becoming sensitive to each other's strengths and weaknesses.

Some of the best games are team games. Just watch the behavior of a group of people divided into two separate teams. The same people who may not have been friends before, when placed on the same team, suddenly won't communicate with anyone but their teammates! They bend over backward to help each other out. They support each other through the duration of the game, and they get to know each other better as well.

A while back, one of my clients ran a team contest called Feed 'Em Beans. For this contest, the winning team was instructed to dress up for a limo ride and a meal at a nice restaurant. They were permitted to order anything they wanted from the menu. The losing team was to dress in very casual clothes for a ride to the same restaurant in an old pickup truck, where they were served water and beans.

During the contest, I visited the store to see how everything was going. Right away, you could sense a difference in the atmosphere. Everyone was pumped up. They were telling me how they had to "get going and figure out what they needed to do to get the job done!" Both teams were scoring and making some very impressive sales. Still, they were constantly challenging themselves to do even better. They wanted to win!

Why Have Games? (What's in It for Me?)

Your answer to the question "Why have games?" is *to improve selling behaviors or sales statistics*. However, as a manager, you need to be aware of games and contests from your sales staff's point of view. Your staff needs to understand that games are set up to benefit the store. And how many teams have performed at their best with no knowledge of their performance—no feedback, no scoreboard, no prize? The answer is *hardly any*.

In all sports, games, and contests, there is a passion for numbers, for the score. There is an intense desire to know how well we did and how well we are doing. Golfers carry their scorecards in their pockets. They mark down each score after each hole played. They compare each score to a previous score on that same hole. They compute whether they're ahead of or behind their previous performance. That's an important part of the game. That's what makes it fun, stimulating, and challenging. The same holds true for the games you run in your store.

Why Get Better if You Don't Keep Score?

I also happen to believe that the prize, the reward or the payoff for achieving a goal—for accomplishing something significant—is very important. I'm not saying that the challenge and the competitiveness needed to accomplish each goal aren't the driving forces—they are. But each prize becomes the symbol of the corresponding achievement. That is *recognition*. And we all like recognition.

Recognition can be money. It can be merchandise. It can be time off with pay. It can be a certificate of merit, a victory medal, or maybe a permanent plaque nailed to a wall in your store with the winner's name engraved on it. You can recognize your staff in a million ways. Whatever the reward, it is a symbol that the salesperson has done something remarkable and worthy of everyone's attention. So, when you plan your contests or games, never forget the celebration—the emotional compensation. It answers that all-important question "What's in it for me?"

CHAPTER TWO

ELEMENTS OF A GAME

Begin with the end in mind.

There's no doubt—it's fun to use games and contests to improve statistics and behaviors. Even so, these activities shouldn't be taken lightly. They are high-performance projects that must be carefully planned. Every successful game or contest I've ever seen was characterized by attention to detail in planning and preparation. Remember that old computer expression, *GIGO*? It means "Garbage In=Garbage Out." The expression I use about games is *PIRO*. It means "Preparation In=Results Out!"

Preparation is essential. I know from experience—a manager who runs games without taking the time to plan them very carefully is making a big mistake. The preparation you put into a game or contest determines the results you get.

A Never-Ending Process

An important part of your job is figuring out how to breathe life into your selling floor on a consistent basis. Setting up games and contests should take up a portion of each week's planning exercises.

Your store needs to have a personality. It needs to have some character. Games and contests can have a significant return on investment for you, your salespeople, and your store. Remember—we're not talking about having contests and games just so you can give away prizes and rewards. This is not a giveaway. You invest your time to get a return in the form of an improved statistic or more effective selling behaviors.

The first thing to consider when you're planning a game or contest is your ultimate goal: What do you want your game or contest to achieve? When you plan your games with the end in mind, they'll be much more successful.

The Elements of a Game: The 10 Commandments

As a guideline, here are 10 essentials for putting a game together. These are basic concepts that are easy to understand and implement.

1. The Game Shall Be Written

Games and contests are intended to provide wonderful opportunities for people to be recognized when they do extraordinary things. Just try to imagine what it must be like for someone who goes that extra mile—who thinks she's won the big prize—to be told, "Sorry, no way!" This can happen when there's confusion over the rules, or when the rules aren't written down.

For me, one of the biggest tragedies in running contests is that the games we use as incentives to motivate people are often not written down, not fully explained, and not fully understood by everyone involved.

The games you run must be clearly laid out for everyone to understand. Each game will be different. Each will have its own process, purpose, and rules. Therefore, all games must be in written form.

Write down the precise details of each game before it starts. Don't make what will happen in one set of circumstances or another a matter of opinion. Get rid of all the gray areas and make everything black and white. You want to avoid any possibility of a misunderstanding or misinterpretation. Write everything down!

Consider:

- How will ties be handled?

- How will the game be tracked?

- How will returns, denied credit, and so on be handled?
- How could salespeople tamper with the results?

2. The Game Shall Have a Goal

Every game should have a single focused goal—one worth achieving. Achieving that goal is success, and the prize for winning the game is the reward. Perhaps the goal will be to increase items per sale or sales per hour by a certain percentage. The goal could even be moving a certain amount of "dead" merchandise out the door.

Whatever your goal or target, make sure it's realistic and attainable. I've seen it again and again—managers new to running games want to really go for it, so they give their salespeople targets that are way out of their range and that they have no chance of winning. I can assure you that it doesn't take salespeople long to figure out they're not going to hit the mark. That is not very motivating. How much fun do you think it is to play a game you can't possibly win?

I'm not suggesting you should set goals that are "gimmes," the kinds of goals that everyone is sure to reach. What I am suggesting is that you develop challenging goals with a little stretch in them. You need the kinds of goals that will get the best from your people—that will be fun for them to shoot for.

3. The Game Shall Have a Specific Timeframe

Is there anything magical about how long a game or contest should run? No. All you have to do is take a look at what people in retailing are most interested in. We all know, for instance, that when looking at numbers, upper management mostly looks at what happens at the end of the year. District managers tend to be more interested in what happens monthly. And, as a member of store management, you're interested in how the numbers look at the end of the week, and then at the end of the month.

Remember: The only reason you run a game or contest is to improve a statistic or a selling behavior.

But what about your salespeople? The ones I've worked with want to know what they did at the end of a day, or at the end of a week. They like getting feedback fast. And since they're the ones who are going to be playing these games, it makes sense that the games be short and sweet. Chances are, they'll lose interest if they have to wait too long to find out if they've done well, or even if they've won something. So, to keep them motivated, you'll want to run daily games, weekend games, and weekly games. This means you're going to have to run a lot of games and contests.

Occasionally, there can be a game that runs longer than a week. If there's a major goal to be accomplished or a major store event being promoted, there can be a monthly game. But games that run longer than a month have to be very special. Those have to be the big ones, with more exciting and expensive rewards.

4. The Game Shall Have Rules
You can't play a game without having some rules to follow. Knowing the rules makes a game easier to play. That's why everyone should know what the rules are. You must explain the rules and make certain everyone follows them.

The rules of each game need to be clearly stated and be accepted by everyone. The rules should include:

- What specifically must be achieved in order to win?

- How will ties be handled?

- How will the game be tracked?

- When will the prizes be awarded?

- How many winners can there be?

- Who is going to play?

- What happens if someone plays dishonestly?

You'll also find that some games have special circumstances that require you to set up some exceptions to the rules.

Suppose you're playing Pass the Buck, in which whoever makes the first sale of the day is given a twenty-dollar bill (or whatever amount you want). The bill is passed along to the next salesperson who makes a larger sale. This goes on all day long, and the person making the largest single sale gets to keep the money at the end of the day.

What happens if the first sale of the day in your store is absolutely gigantic? According to the rules, you'll give the person who made that sale the prize first thing in the morning. Is that a problem? It could be, if the likelihood of that prize being passed along to anyone else is pretty slim.

No one is going to want to play a game and do their best when there's no chance of winning. In order to get around this problem, you'll have to make exceptions to the rules now and then so the game can continue. It's important to stay flexible. If there's a rule that's ruining a game, fix it—don't enforce it!

5. The Game Shall Be Tracked

There should be a constant reminder that a game is in progress. Show that something's happening by using posters, banners, streamers, a contest board—anything that will create the spirit and excitement of competition. You want everyone to be consciously aware that there's a contest or a game going on.

You'll need to decide how often you will actually track the results. You could keep everyone in suspense and total up the results at the end of each day. Or you could build a competitive atmosphere by keeping a running count as the day, weekend, or week progresses.

You'll want to decide how and where you'll track the results. Will you use a gigantic game board with tally marks? Or a corkboard with a lot of colored pushpins? I've even seen a game tracked on a large jigsaw puzzle, where a picture or a word is formed when the pieces are filled in by the salespeople who are reaching goals. Each of the pieces has a special mark showing who put it there. At a glance, everyone playing the game knows how they're measuring up against the competition.

The point is that by visually tracking a game, you're also promoting it—constantly. You're reminding everyone that something is going on. By making sure your tracking is highly visible, you'll be calling attention to the contest every single time someone sees that game board, that poster, that puzzle, or that sign. This is exciting and fun, and it keeps the momentum building.

Get your salespeople involved in the tracking process—give them something to do! When they've achieved something that earns them points or prizes, let them be the ones to move the pushpin, log the information, or ring the bell. Let them be part of the whole thing. Make it their production.

For example, we have a poker card game that's been very successful. It gets people really involved. When someone makes a sale or sells an add-on, that person gets to draw a card—this is done right away. Each time someone draws a card, that person knows he or she has achieved something. The more cards a person is able to draw, the better his or her chances of getting a good poker hand. And, of course, the best poker hand wins.

But the big motivator here isn't whether a salesperson wins a poker hand. The real motivation is in just getting a chance to try. When a salesperson draws another card, his or her success can be seen by everyone. This stimulates competition and keeps the spirit of the game alive.

6. The Game Shall Have Props
Whenever possible, use the genuine articles called for when playing a game. They add realism, credibility, and authenticity. I can't tell you how many times I've seen games played with phony money. *Never use phony money!* Phony money isn't real, isn't exciting to look at, and has no value. There's nothing motivating about phony money. When we play Pass the Buck, we give our salespeople real money and tell them not to put the money in their pockets. "Don't hide it! Pin that bill right on your jacket, where everyone can see it!" It's fun. It's the prize! And it's real.

If you're running a game that's designed around a sport, such as baseball, bowling, golf, or football, get some props that are used in the sport. Set the right mood and create an authentic atmosphere. Keep it fun. Make it different! If the game is designed around a game board or a puzzle with pieces, build one—and build it to scale. Make sure your salespeople can see the numbers on the board. Make sure they can see the pictures of the prizes on the wheel. Make it work!

Finally, you can tap into current events and have a lot of fun. We once had a contest using *Jurassic Park* as the theme, with miniature dinosaurs, extinction pits, and a game board that was filled with all sorts of interesting challenges.

7. The Game Shall Have Appropriate Rewards

Everyone loves prizes—the more, the better! But everyone is different, and the only sure way to know what kinds of rewards are best is to experiment. If your salespeople achieve the goal you've set, be it the higher statistic or the improved selling behavior, your reward is most likely a good one. If they don't achieve your goal, then the reward may not have done the job, or your goal was not achievable, and you should decide on alternatives. Curiously enough, one surefire way of selecting a good reward is simply to ask your salespeople what they want. Give them some options, such as:

- A specific amount of cash

- Dinner/gift certificates

- No housekeeping duties for a week

- Concert/sporting-event tickets

- Extended employee discounts

Mix up the types of rewards. Try everything from cash to merchandise to special kinds of prizes. If you've got a game running that's about baseball, then get some baseball tickets. Show some creativity. To help you out, I've included a list in the back of the book of small, medium, and large prizes that my clients have used successfully through the years.

8. Everyone Shall Have an Opportunity to Win

I don't like the idea of just one winner. Every now and then, with something like Pass the Buck, it's fun to have one winner. However, no *sustained* game should have just one winner. This is because your most skilled salespeople—your most experienced and your best—will always win. The odds are definitely in their favor and everyone knows it.

Successful games are ones where all the salespeople think they have an opportunity to win, not just the stars and the high performers. A game shouldn't be a sure thing or "in the bag" for anyone. You must think of ways to give all your people an equal opportunity to win. Percentage increases over individual past performance can get that accomplished in a hurry. An equal chance to win is another good reason for having team games. These games always produce multiple winners and at the same time create an unbelievable degree of competitiveness on the selling floor.

9. The Game Shall Have Leadership

This is an important element. I know that throughout the process of a game or contest, salespeople may go through a phase of disenchantment. There's always the possibility the game you're running has not worked the way you thought it would. And, of course, there can be lots of reasons why things don't happen the way you want them to. So, what do you do—apologize and call off the game?

That's not a good idea. Credibility is one of the most difficult characteristics to earn. It's very fragile. It takes a long time to earn, and can be so easily lost. And once it's gone, you'll have a real uphill battle trying to get it back again. Games should never be stopped once they are started. Even if you reach the conclusion that your game isn't working, play it through to the end anyway. No one should stop in the middle of a game. If anything, heighten your commitment. Show everyone you're still supporting their efforts. Let some enthusiasm show.

10. The Game Shall Give a Return on Investment

Your time is very valuable, and so are the financial resources of your company. Well-run companies look very carefully at all the things they invest in. You should also look very carefully at the time you invest in creating and running these games, and what it will cost on the downside. And although I strongly urge you to run as many contests and games as you can come up with, never forget your reason for being on the sales floor, and that is to sell!

PIRO! Preparation In—Results Out!

First, decide what you want to accomplish—your goal for each game. You need to know what the end result should look like, because if you don't know, you won't get there. Then carefully think through each game. Work through these 10 commandments, and make sure that your games will give you the results you want.

CHAPTER THREE

SELLING THE GAME TO YOUR STAFF

You can't light a fire with a wet match.

Have you ever told what you thought was a great joke, and nobody laughed? Or written and delivered a great speech, with a lot of important information in it, and nobody listened? This happens to all of us, and I can tell you that I am the champion. When this happens to you, no matter what the situation, you have to continue to give it your all. This is essential.

Selling a game or contest to your staff is no different. You're a professional, and when you're in front of your staff, you're on stage. Whatever your staff's reaction to a contest, a game, or any event, you must be excited and stay excited. You'll never ignite a fire if you don't set off some sparks. Your enthusiasm has to be contagious; it needs to spread like a bonfire. Why? Because you can't run the store and hit your store's sales goals alone. It takes all of your staff to get extraordinary things done. Selling the game to your staff is all about getting individuals to work together toward a common goal.

Share Your Vision
Selling the game means showing your people that there can be something special about the work they may see as dull and repetitious. You must find that extra something for your salespeople, something that goes beyond the ordinary, something that's going to lift everyone's spirits and add a little pizzazz to the job.

Imagine the game in progress. Visualize it working in your store, with everyone enjoying the challenge and the competition—and a positive end result. And then, believe that what is merely a picture in your own mind can become the real thing!

Now it's time to share your vision with your staff. You'll need to plan out how you will share your vision, how you will get your staff excited about each game or contest. This is why I think the whole *PIRO* concept—Preparation In, Results Out—is so important for a successful game. Let me tell you a great PIRO story:

A store manager named Sam loved using games. He called me and told me he was getting ready to run a new game designed around a horse-racing theme. He asked if I'd come out to his store when he announced the game to his staff. I said, "Of course!"

Only the salespeople were at the store when I arrived. After a few minutes, in walked Sam, dressed up as a jockey! He made a grand entrance wearing shiny black boots, a bright-red-checkered cap, a red silk shirt, jodhpurs, and, yes, the goggles, too. He threw a CD into a player and you heard the bugle music that you hear when the horses parade onto the track. Then, he immediately started selling everyone on the new game.

The success with which people are able to influence, persuade, or inspire others depends on their ability to connect with people emotionally. Sam connected emotionally and sold the game to his staff.

Show Personal Conviction
The greatest obstacle managers can meet when attempting to sell a game to their staff is their inability to demonstrate their own personal conviction. As a manager, you need to ask yourself, "Am I running this game to do something, or am I running this game just for something to do?" You will never convince others to share in your commitment if you're not convinced of it yourself. What does it take to show this commitment?

Actions speak louder than words. We've all heard that before, but what does it really mean? What kinds of actions are we talking about?

The first action is personal involvement in the game. You can't just sit in the bleachers and watch the game being played. Just being a spectator doesn't show much of a commitment or any real involvement. Now, we're not talking about you actively playing the game. You can't take the ball and run with it, leaving your people to follow along as best as they can. That isn't the kind of personal involvement that's going to prove to your people that you're supporting them and want them to achieve results.

Your involvement in the game should focus on giving your people the enthusiasm to perform at their best. You need to reinforce their desire to do well and to grow as they become more successful—to do their thing. Be their coach and their cheerleader. Get personally involved in their efforts to succeed. Be there to talk with them about game strategies. Give them feedback about their efforts and their performance.

If you want, use a microphone to broadcast individual or team successes and milestones that deserve recognition as they are achieved. Blast it!

When the game is over, share the results and talk about what everyone might have done differently or better.

Be the coach when the game is being played.

This kind of personal involvement and participation will demonstrate the importance you place on playing the game. When your people see that you're taking the time to be that involved—continuously, consistently, and enthusiastically—your credibility will soar. So will your staff's interest in playing the game. They will want to do their best and achieve the kind of results you're after.

Avoid Familyosity

I've coined a word—*familyosity*—to describe a condition that develops most frequently in small environments, but can develop in large ones, too.

Familyosity refers to a group of people who've been working together for a such a long time that business formality between them has almost disappeared. They're family; they're friends. They play it nice and loose with each other. And often, they let things slide.

Let's say that Bob is one of my employees. He's a key player on my staff, and we've worked together for a number of years. We get along great; we're like family. Now, if he comes in late every now and then, or puts off finishing an assignment, should I make a big deal over it? After all, he's family, isn't he?

This is familyosity, the idea that working partners become an extended family that follows a different set of rules. A lot of us at The Friedman Group have worked together for many years. Could there be any formality left between us? Absolutely! There can be a tremendous amount when it's appropriate. That's because we all have responsibilities and duties to perform—and none of us, myself included, should be able to slide just because we've been here a few years and know each other well.

I believe that at each level of every company there are specific jobs each person must perform if goals are to be met. Familyosity contributes to an environment that allows people to not do their jobs. Familyosity destroys the competitive spirit we want so much to create.

For example, suppose two people have been working in your store for a few years. They get along very well, have become friends, and are comfortable working with each other. One day, you announce, "We're going to play a game. We're going to have a contest!" What is their response? "A game? What are you talking about? What do we need to play a game for? It's silly! We've been here too long to have to do things like that!"

Obviously, these two people are not comfortable with the idea of having to compete. They're not comfortable with the idea of having to measure up—of being held accountable. After all, you know what they can do. You've known them both a long time. Why should they have to prove anything? They consider themselves family and expect you to excuse them from participating in the game.

This is the time for you to establish yourself as the leader in your store, as someone who gets things done. Your staff needs to know that when they show up for work, you are the leader. If there's a game going on, they're expected to play it. And everyone is expected to give it his or her all.

Identify the Challenging Opportunities

Although games and contests are incredibly motivating, there's still something about them that seems to move certain people right out of their comfort zone.

It's pretty easy to identify these people. They don't want to participate. They have an "I can't do it" or "Why should I do it?" attitude. Over the years, I've found that to be really good at selling games to your staff, you need to figure out what it's going to take to get these people into the "Let's have some fun and I'll do the best I can" zone.

I think people who are reluctant to play fall into two categories. First, there are the Protesters. They're the ones who generally knock the idea of playing games. They ridicule games by saying, "They're dumb!" Then there's another group I call the Quitters. They give up. They don't see themselves as competitive and the whole idea of vying for something is stressful to them. It may seem that these people have different reasons for not wanting to play the game. But if you take a closer look, you'll see that their motives are pretty much the same. People have a tendency to either criticize or run away from what they think they can't do well.

That's human nature. Here's an example: A salesperson named Marie announces that the game is a waste of time. Or maybe Marie mentions that she never has been good at playing games. Marie plays the game and loses. Do you think anyone's going to have the impression she was even trying? They're going to think the only reason she lost the game was because she didn't care about winning. And they'll be right.

Let's look at another example of this tendency not to care about winning when we don't think we'll do well. Anyone who knows me can appreciate how much I like to play games. I'm very competitive and love the idea of being in any kind of a contest. I'll play a game anytime and anywhere. This is especially true on business trips. As soon as the business formalities of the day are over I'll try to find a reason to get people together and orchestrate something like playing miniature golf, bowling, or a card game. I love the socialization process.

On one particular business trip, we decided to go bowling. One of my trainers, Michele, wasn't that interested in bowling. It's not a big deal to her. She wasn't very enthusiastic and didn't care how well she did. She said, "Harry, I don't bowl a lot. I'm not good at it, and I really don't care if I shoot 80, 90, or 100."

There it was. She was telling me, in advance, that she wasn't good at it, she didn't care, and she wasn't even going to try. After listening to what Michele had to say, I took her aside and shared something with her. I said, "Look, Michele—we all agreed to come down here and bowl. Like it or not, we're here to play three games. Now, whether you like to bowl or not, you have to admit that all of us being here together is fun. Right?" She agreed.

"Then why," I added, "wouldn't you want to bowl the very best you can? Why not concentrate and try to knock down some pins? Maybe you can even get a strike! And if you just happened to land one, wouldn't that be more fun than just getting gutter balls?" Of course it would. "Wouldn't it be more fun to be the very best bowler you can humanly be, just for tonight? I'm not asking you to go bowling tomorrow, and I don't really care whether you ever go bowling again. But you're here tonight, and since you're here, why not give it the best you can? Why not play the game all the way? At least give it a try!"

The point I was trying to make with Michele is that it's a terrible waste of time to not want to try. How many people say to themselves, "I'm not good at this," or "That isn't what I'm interested in"? What an empty use of time in their lives. They're creating a wasteland of unused opportunities for getting better and stretching themselves. It's so unfortunate. It's so dull. There's no adventure in their lives, and there's no fun.

I believe that you can bring a new, competitive spirit to your people. When you hear the Protesters and the Quitters make remarks like "Add-ons just aren't my thing" or "I never win at games," say, "Look, you show up for work every single day—why not try to get better? Why not have higher sales at the end of the day? You're going to be here anyway."

I also believe that even people who complain about participating love the idea of belonging to something. Most everyone likes being part of a group. When we have a choice between being on the outside or the inside, most of us would choose the inside. Games and contests will get those people involved, on the inside, if you give them a reason to do so.

Protesters and Quitters need to be reminded that in life things either get better or worse. Change is constant. Time goes by. They can't get it back once it's gone. They have to do something with it now. So, when it's time to play the game, tell them to use that time to accomplish something worthwhile, to use that time to make themselves feel better as people, to use that time to learn new things and develop new skills—and above all, in whatever they do, to do it the best they can!

There's a special point I have to mention here. It's one of those exceptions to the rules. If you have some top producers—some real stars—who don't want to visibly take an active part in the game, you may consider leaving them alone. I'm talking about the ones in your store who are regularly over sales goals and constantly giving you what you want. If these salespeople are continually coming through for you with their sales statistics, don't make their lack of participation an issue. These top performers will excel with or without the contest or game. Just make sure they understand that they are not to spoil it for the others. For the game to be a success, the others must feel motivated and excited.

Establish High Expectations
There's an old cliché, "It's not whether you win or lose, but how you play the game." I hate clichés, especially when they're not appropriate or correct. The point of that saying is simple: if you play the game properly and give it your all, what happens after that just happens. You've made the effort, and that's all that counts.

This may sound fine, but it doesn't work that way in the real world. I'll never be convinced that any salesperson is going to get any satisfaction out of losing all the time. Your salespeople don't come to work each day with a compelling impulse to lose. They want to win! And it's your job to inspire them to do their very best. Set high expectations for your staff.

If we never make mistakes, we never learn.

You also need to get the message across to each of your people that he or she can win, individually, just by trying to get better. Make clear to your staff that what you'd like to see is some movement in the right direction.

Games and contests with targets give people great opportunities to go for something—to get better. Of course, to do this means having the courage to take some risks, and not being afraid to make some mistakes.

Yes, that's what I said: You want to let your people know you expect them to make mistakes, and that it's okay to make mistakes. Sure, it's frustrating to make mistakes. But mistakes give us opportunities to say, "What happened here? What did I do wrong? What can I learn from this experience?"

Start thinking about some of the most famous winners in history—you'll see that the only way they were able to improve themselves was to fall down every now and then. If they hadn't pushed themselves to try anything new or difficult, if their only objective had been to play it safe by not falling down, they wouldn't have improved. They wouldn't have accomplished anything.

Take Babe Ruth, for instance. Babe Ruth is considered probably the greatest slugger in baseball history. People remember the records he set, including his 714 regular-season home runs. But how many people know that he struck out over 1,300 times trying to reach that mark? Can you imagine how his fans reacted to seeing him strike out—especially with men on base? But the Babe knew he'd never hit a home run unless he tried.

That's what you want your people to do in every game and contest you run. You want them to try.

One final thought about selling the game: It's all about getting people to work together, and that's everything. The fundamental principle "You are only as good as your people make you" has stood the test of time. A one-person football team isn't going to get very far and will certainly result in losses. There's no way you can make your store successful all by yourself. It's going to take everyone working together to achieve a common goal.

Have a game plan beforehand, get excited about that plan, and stay excited! If you're involved, your salespeople will be involved. I'm convinced that there's no limit to how much their sales will rise once you get the involvement, the enthusiasm, and the commitment of your staff.

CHAPTER FOUR

MAKING YOUR CASE AND ESTABLISHING A REWARD SYSTEM

Make an offer they can't refuse.

If you could prove the return on investment you'd get from running contests and games, there would be very few retail store owners who wouldn't want to give you the money to run those games. It's inconceivable that you'd be denied that extra money if you convinced management that it's worth it. So, convincing management that it's worth it becomes a very important part of your job.

A short time ago, a client asked me for help when he'd had no luck getting extra money for his games and contests.

"My basic problem, Harry," he said, "is that they just don't seem to care. They're not interested in how much fun it would be for everyone in the store. I keep telling them how dull and repetitious selling can get, and how much more exciting and interesting everyone's jobs would be if we just had a contest or a game going on! But it's like talking to a brick wall!"

He couldn't understand why management didn't care whether the people in his store had fun. He couldn't see why management showed no interest in having him do things like games to make working in the store more exciting and more interesting.

He didn't understand it. But I did—completely!

Retailers will not be persuaded to run contests just so everyone can have a good time. Furthermore, they're not going to think it's a smart idea for you to spend valuable time planning and running games just to provide your people with a more interesting and exciting environment. And they're certainly not going to get very excited about running games if all you want to do is give away their money!

You're going to have to prove to them that these activities will provide a return on investment, and not just be a giveaway. Management wants to hear you say that you want to run games and contests to improve sales statistics or selling behaviors. And when they give you the green light to go ahead and run a game, they're going to want to be shown the return on their investment.

The only reason you run a game or a contest is to improve a sales statistic or a selling behavior.

Getting Game and Contest Money

I'm aware that most retail stores have little or no budget for game prizes and rewards. A little later in this chapter, I'll introduce you to our Game Authorization Form, which we've developed to help you define your game elements in black and white—to make getting authorization easier.

But before you get to the authorization process, the money must be allocated to spend. We have developed three sample formulas for getting game and contest money. (Of course, these are just ideas.)

Formula #1

This formula is very good for generating small amounts of money. It's called The Evergreen Plan, because it is perpetual and endless.

- Determine a percentage of sales to be used for game money, based on whatever your sales were the previous year in exactly the same time period you plan to run the game.

- After you have calculated that amount, you may either spend that money or carry it forward and add it to the amount resulting from the same percentage of sales for the game period that follows.

For instance, suppose that in the first week of August last year, you did $10,000. For the purpose of our example, we'll use 0.1 percent as our game-money percentage. If you take 0.1 percent of $10,000, you have $10 to spend on a game or contest ($10,000 multiplied by 0.001).

But maybe that's not enough. Maybe for the particular game you have in mind, you want a little more money. So, carry that amount forward to what's available in the following week and add that amount to the $10 for a larger payoff.

Here's an example of how this works:

LY August Sales Week #1	LY August Sales Week #2	LY August Sales Week #3	LY August Sales Week #4	0.1%	$ for the Game
$10,000				$10.00	$10.00
	$14,000			$14.00	$24.00
		$12,750			
			$10,850		

The amount of money that you can generate for your games using this formula is nonstop and uninterrupted.

Formula #2

The philosophy inherent in this formula is that the amount of money budgeted and spent is directly related to sums above and beyond expected sales increases.

- Determine the amount your store did last year within a specific timeframe (e.g., a week, a month, etc.).

- Determine the goal you want to achieve this year.

- After the results are in, determine the dollar amount your store did above and beyond your goal figure.

- Subtract the cost of goods from that number.

- Determine a specific percentage (e.g., 20 percent) of that number. This is the amount of money you now have for a game.

This formula can generate larger amounts of money than The Evergreen Plan. It's a good and fair formula because you're only getting a percentage of the amount over and above what you wanted to achieve in the first place. Here's an example of how it works:

LY August Sales Week #1	$ to Reach Goal	Actual	Incremental Increase	Less Cost of Goods (50%)	$ for the Game (20%)
$10,000	$12,000	$14,000	$2,000	$1,000	$200.00

LY August Sales Week #2	$ to Reach Goal	Actual	Incremental Increase	Less Cost of Goods (50%)	$ for the Game (20%)
$14,000	$16,000	$16,200	$200	$100	$20.00

This same formula can be used for games and contests where individuals have set certain goals for themselves. Their rewards would be 20 percent of the amount above and beyond their goals.

Let's say you're going to have a contest based on last year's individual statistics for each person in your store. Carole did $3,500 last year, Jim did $4,200, and Sue did $5,100.

This is how it might look:

Employee	LY November Week #1	$ to Reach Goal	Actual/ Incremental Increase	Less Cost of Goods (50%)	20% of Gross Profit = Reward
Carole	$3,500	$4,700	$5,900 ($4,700) $1,200	$600	$600 × 0.20 = $120.00
Jim	$4,200	$4,700	$6,300 ($4,700) $1,600	$800	$800 × 0.20 = $160.00
Sue	$5,100	$4,700	$6,100 ($4,700) $1,400	$700	$700 × 0.20 = $140.00
TOTALS	**$12,800**	**$14,100**	**$18,300**	**$2,100**	**$420.00**

Here is the million-dollar question: Would an owner give away $420 if he thought he could do $18,300? If he thought he could do $5,500 more than he did the year before? Of course he would! You shouldn't get any argument from management when you can produce these kinds of numbers.

Formula #3

With this formula, the amount to be spent on games is determined in the budget. A certain amount of money is budgeted each year as a marketing or advertising expense.

After all, games and contests are really internal marketing. There is always money in the budget for advertising and for beautiful displays and promotions. But it's the people who actually sell. And it's the managers who create the environment in which these people are excited and eager to sell.

The intelligent, entrepreneurial owner of a store understands that you can do more business if you can inspire your salespeople to sell. And it's the games and contests you run that will inspire your salespeople and cause them to do extraordinary things!

Game Authorization Form

Once the money is allocated, you can't just go to management and say, "I want some money to run a contest in my store." No good businessperson is going to hand over money to you without knowing exactly how you want to spend it and why. That's why we created the Game Authorization Form. If you come up with a good game or a contest and orchestrate it very well, you should be able to go to management with this form and get approval for the money to run the game.

We believe most companies will authorize a game that will improve a sales statistic or a selling behavior if the game is written up properly. The write-up must justify that the money is worth spending.

That's the purpose of our Game Authorization Form. It's formal documentation used to gain access to money available for the game. Writing up a Game Authorization Form is a formal process that helps managers think through some of the aspects of the game or contest, describing how and why running the game will benefit the company. The major issues addressed are:

1. What is the purpose or goal of the contest/game?

"To increase last year's sales by 10 percent."

2. How will the contest/game work?

"Salespeople will be divided into teams. The object of the game is for teams to compete against each other and achieve the largest total volume of sales. The team that produces the greatest volume of sales wins the prizes."

3. What are the start and end dates?

"Game will start on February 12 and end on February 14. It will last three days."

4. How will the results be measured?

"Each hour, the manager will tally the total dollar volume of sales produced by each team. A bell will sound, alerting everyone that the hourly tally is being made. The captain of each team will move the team's marker to the appropriate spot on the game board that shows how each team compares to the other in sales production. A red line on the game board will signify the actual target. Any sales volume produced that goes beyond that point is over and above the goal. Each team that moves beyond that red line is in bonus territory. This added dimension gives both teams a chance to win."

5. What are the rewards (and consequences, if any)?

"The individuals on the team that produces the greatest sales volume will be the outright winners, and will each be awarded gift certificates of equal value. All salespeople on either team who pass the red line will win a bonus prize of extended employee discounts."

6. What are the costs of the contest/game?

"Gift certificates will have a value of $30.00 each. No more than four of these certificates will be issued. Extended employee discounts of 20 percent for a one-time buy will be awarded to the members of each team that produces sales over and above the 10 percent goal."

As you can see, the primary ingredients of the Game Authorization Form are similar to the issues we addressed in Chapter 2, "Elements of a Game."

STORE CONTEST/GAME AUTHORIZATION FORM

Requested by: _____ Store # _____ Date _____

What is the purpose of the contest/game? _____
_____
_____

How will the contest/game work? _____
_____
_____
_____
_____

Start Date: _____   End Date: _____
How will the results be measured? _____
_____
_____
_____
_____

What are the rewards (and consequences, if any)? _____
_____
_____
_____

Cost of contest/game? _____
Approved Signature _____
Comments: _____
_____
_____
_____
_____

Your success at convincing management that games and contests are worth the extra money will depend on knowing in advance what you are trying to accomplish, thinking through how it will be done, and then having a method for tracking the results.

You also need to let management know what you want to use for rewards. This part of the planning process should be given careful attention. The rewards you choose should boost the energy level of your salespeople enough to be beneficial. They have to have some value to your staff. But a reward doesn't always have to be money.

In the game Pass the Buck, for example, you could pass an extended employee discount, pass a day off with pay, pass an extra-long lunch, pass no housekeeping duties for one week, and so forth. The emphasis should always be on recognizing accomplishments. Rewards symbolize movement in the right direction and provide a stamp of approval and encouragement to continue the effort.

Finally, you need to predict how much the game is going to cost and then estimate what you think will be the return on investment. Will the potential benefits (increase in sales) outweigh the risks (actual costs)? This is an important step that you should never forget. When the game is over, you can see whether your return is what you thought it would be, and figure out ways to improve your game planning for next time.

Different Kinds of Rewards

Now that you have the money for the game, it's time to select the rewards. I think you'll agree that getting extraordinary results from games and contests doesn't just happen. Every contest and game you run should be treated as something special. They should be significant events.

Earlier, we talked briefly about what might be considered the most appropriate rewards. Of course, knowing this with absolute and precise accuracy means being able to get inside the minds of your people and finding out what they value most. The problem is, everyone's different. We're all motivated by different things. Obviously, then, we have to go with things we think will work.

Rewards to use in games and contests fall into three different categories: *cash rewards*, *merchandise rewards*, and *non-monetary rewards*.

Whatever the rewards, have some fun when you give them away! Make it dramatic and thrilling. Choreograph and orchestrate it from the very beginning.

We ran a contest with a client a few years back that involved rewarding people with large sums of money. To make the event really dramatic, the president of the company announced the game by walking in with a briefcase handcuffed to his wrists. Two security guards accompanied him. He pulled a key out of his pocket and opened up the briefcase. It was filled with money—real money. It looked like there were thousands and thousands of dollars. The impact of showing people in advance what they could win was phenomenal. And that was just the beginning.

After the game was over, when it was time to give out the money, the president did the same thing. He walked in with that same briefcase, the handcuffs, and the security guards. He opened the briefcase and started to announce the winners. One person won $900! The president could have just handed that person a check and said "Congratulations!" and everyone would have clapped and smiled and shaken his hand. The excitement would have lasted only a few seconds.

Instead, the president took a handful of money from the briefcase and began peeling off $100 bills. And each time he peeled off one of those bills, he counted, "One hundred, two hundred, three hundred . . . ." Then everyone started counting along with him—it was incredible! The company gave away over $5,000 in that contest, and the sales that month went through the ceiling. It was an explosion! And it was fun.

Keep the momentum going as long as you can. Just because the game is over, don't be in a hurry to bury it as old business. Milk it and make it a memorable experience so no one will forget. You want your staff to talk about the game afterward, and laugh about it, too.

Cash Rewards

We can safely say that most people like money. A cash reward is always appealing. It's one of the things that will always make people light up. Cash is something people like because they're able to pay their bills with it. They can use cash to buy exactly what they want. So, never worry about whether people will appreciate receiving money—they will.

But if you can, it's important to give them *cash*—not checks. If you announce the prize is $100, don't give the winner a check for $86.23 because you had to deduct taxes. Your people have worked hard for some recognition. They're craving it. It's Showtime, and they want to see lights blinking and hear bells ringing. They're waiting for some recognition, and they're all ready to celebrate. And you're deducting taxes? Where's the fun in that?

Why not reduce what you plan to give away and pay the taxes yourself? Offer up less in the contest so you can give out rewards in cash, and give the bookkeeping part of all this to your accountant. And if your accountant can't figure out how to give cash to your salespeople—get another accountant!

Merchandise Rewards
Money is only one of the things that get people to light up and take notice. Prizes do, too. And prizes can be great incentives, especially if they're things your people really want and they're given away dramatically—with some flair. Orchestrate the award process so that your people connect with their rewards emotionally. Make it fun. Make it last. Make it memorable!

There are a lot of people who work in certain kinds of retail stores only because they love the activity associated with the kind of merchandise they sell. They're hiking enthusiasts or bicyclists. They're tennis players and golf nuts. And they're crazy about the merchandise they sell. Selling just happens to be a byproduct of something they love very much.

Now, pretend you're the manager of a store specializing in fitness equipment. Can you imagine the fire you'd light under your people if you announced, "These home gyms are going to belong to every single person who can reach his or her goal this month!"

When you tantalize people with the idea that they can actually own that home gym, or those tents they want, or that camping equipment or tennis racket they need, or that they could ride those bicycles or play a round of golf at Pebble Beach—just by reaching a target—they'll go crazy!

A couple of years ago, one of my scuba-diving store clients decided to run a big weekend contest using a point system. With this type of system, salespeople earn a certain number of points every time they achieve a performance goal.

Weeks in advance of the contest, the manager shopped some of her neighboring retail stores. She told them she was putting on this contest and wanted to buy some of their merchandise as prizes. Naturally, she was able to get everything at a discount.

After all of the merchandise was accumulated, she displayed everything in her break room and tagged each item with a point value. Once the room was all set up, she announced the game. She invited everyone to come in and look around at the merchandise, and then she distributed the rule sheet. The rule sheet outlined, among other things, how to earn points to buy the merchandise that was displayed.

Performance Goal	Points
Each sale in excess of $50.00	100
Each sale in excess of $100.00	150
Each sale in excess of $150.00	200
Each sale in excess of $200.00	300
Each sale in excess of $250.00	500
Each sale in excess of $300.00	750

I knew she was running this game, so I went by her store a few hours after the game started. This was the same working environment I had seen the week before—nothing physically had changed. And the salespeople were showing their customers the same merchandise, too—nothing new there, either. Nothing had changed—but everything was different! Sure, I expected to see a certain amount of competition out there. But what I saw was astonishing! These people were really trying to outperform each other for those points. Their adrenaline was pumping.

This manager was very clever. She didn't just tell her salespeople about the prizes, or show them blown-up photographs, either. She took the time to go out and buy prizes in advance. She put the items on display so everyone could look at them, touch them, and get a feeling for what it would be like to own them. She said, "Look here! You want any of these things? They're yours! You can take any of these items home with you Sunday night. But first, you have to go out there and earn them!"

When this contest was over, her statistics were way up. Some people earned enough points to buy more than one prize. Some people wanted the same thing. So, she went out and bought the extra prizes. This is what running games is all about! The game was fun, and it was financially worth it.

The same game was run again the following year. This time, though, it was a lot more elaborate. The manager had a catalog printed, illustrating the prizes and their point values. She put up a tent in the parking lot to display the prizes. Some of the other retailers got involved, too, which made for a real carnival atmosphere. This time the contest lasted a month—and it was even more successful.

One of the interesting things I learned from this experience was that the salespeople were really motivated by using this point system. They said it gave them the chance to get something they probably wouldn't have gone out and bought themselves. Plus, every time they used the prize they had bought with their points, they'd always remember how they earned it. That seemed very important to them. I thought this was significant.

Using a point system is outstanding for games and contests, because the salespeople are always searching for ways to increase their point totals in order to pick out more elaborate gifts. They're stretching themselves all the time. And the best part of using a point system is that more than one person can win! Anyone who gives it all they've got and achieves some personal bests will be rewarded.

Vendor Involvement

Don't fail to tap into your vendors for products and merchandise. They can get involved in a really big way, but only for very special occasions.

With a vendor's participation, you can really score on a promotional contest where you're trying to push a particular item. In these games, whoever sells the most units of a particular computer or a certain stereo set gets a special prize, such as a trip to Hawaii. The vendor pays for the trip—and gladly.

Now, let's consider a different kind of arrangement. Say you manage a jewelry store and want to run a special promotion on a particular watch. This is a beautiful watch that just about any salesperson would want to win. So, how about going to your vendor and saying, "I want to run a promotional contest on this watch all week long. And I want the person who sells more of these watches than anyone else to get one. Now, I normally pay you $400 for this watch. Will you give me a better deal on one watch? On the watch that's going to be the big prize?" Of course!

Non-monetary Rewards

It's not necessary to use expensive incentives every time you run a game. Every now and then you might want to come up with some rewards, some incentives, that are free or at least inexpensive. These rewards could include time off with pay, extended employee discounts, parking spaces, a symbolic toy medal, and so on. Even without the money and the expensive prizes, the natural competitive spirit in the people playing can still be the driving force. But you have to remember to create a climate in which your people will do anything for the recognition of just winning!

"What's in It for Me?"

The ultimate challenge, the fundamental part of every game, can be expressed by the words "Bet you can't!" We agree selling is very repetitious. We agree that sooner or later it gets boring. So, when you toss a "Bet you can't!" out onto the selling floor, you fill the air with intensity. By challenging people, you motivate them to want to do their best, even if it's only to win a parking space, a small pin, or an inconsequential button.

By providing people with opportunities to feel a sense of accomplishment and achievement, you're giving them reasons to take pride in what they're doing. What better payoff can there be than that?

The Auction

One example that shows just how strong an impact contests and games can have on sales involves a game called The Auction. A client of mine, a chain of jewelry stores, wanted to increase overall gross sales. They set some lofty goals and then planned a big meeting to get everyone's commitment and start the ball rolling.

I knew achieving these goals was important to them. So, I asked the owners, "If every store in your chain were to exceed its goal, what would you pay? Would you pay $2,000? $3,000? $4,000?" Sure they would. There was no question about it.

I came up with the idea of The Auction. I showed management what I thought could be accomplished with this game, and described how it would work. They gave me the green light.

I invited the managers from each store in the chain to attend a meeting. At the meeting, I put all their names on a board and asked them to call out the sales goals they were assigned. I wrote those numbers next to their names. Then I asked them: "Who thinks they can do better than that? Who'd be willing to increase their goal?" I pointed to a name on the board with a $50,000 goal and said, "Can you do better than that?" I looked around the room and heard, way in the back, "Maybe." Now, of course, everyone turned around. "Sure," the manager said, with more conviction. "I'll bet I can do $62,000!"

The Auction was underway! "You can?" I answered. "Okay! If you can do $12,000 more than your goal, I'll give you $300 in cash. And I'll tell you something else. You can do anything you want with that $300. You can give it out to your people, you can take them to lunch, you can buy prizes for store games—anything you want!"

That got everyone's attention. The door was wide open now. It was Showtime, and everybody got into the act. The higher the managers bet they could go over goal, the more money I committed to giving them. The increases became extraordinary. All the managers were bidding.

After all the numbers were out, I said, "Now let's play real hardball. Who wants to change their bid? Who thinks they can do even more over their goal?"

Why did I do that? As the bidding got hotter and hotter, the managers got more and more aggressive in their bidding. Those who really got into it were promised a lot more money. They knew that the more increases they committed to making, the more money they would get. And so it started all over again. It was exciting. The bidding war went on and on, and the managers kept increasing the amounts over their goals. "I can do that! I can do that, too!"

Once the final bids were in and everything was written down, the question was: Were they dreaming? Could they really do it? Was there enough adrenaline pumping through these managers' veins to keep the momentum going? There wasn't a person in that room who wasn't anxious to get back to his stores and get the process going.

It turned out their enthusiasm carried over to their staff. We gave away $1,500. We had budgeted to give away $6,000. In other words, if everyone had done what they said (or bid), we would have given away $6,000. But we gave away $1,500, which means that a lot of stores went over goal. Was that a good return on investment? You bet!

Some Final Thoughts Before the Games Begin

I'm convinced that having games and contests going on all the time is everything. Successful companies do it day in and day out. It can become a reason for salespeople to come to work each day.

In my company, we'll bet on anything, including the time of day! Ask any person in my company, "What time is it?" If they say anything but "It's Showtime," it costs them $25!

What about trying to show up at one of our company meetings without wearing a Showtime lapel pin? If anyone spots you not wearing it, it's going to cost you $5! I've seen some of my people go crazy trying to see whether someone's wearing their Showtime pin.

There's always a contest, always some game. Something's happening all the time. Because that's who I am, and who we are. That's our personality. Anyone who walks into my company can feel the vitality.

Giving your store a personality and some character is probably 20 percent of your job. And that's what games do for a store. Customers hate walking into somber stores filled with gloom and silence—the kind of store where you can hear a pin drop. Customers can't wait to get out of stores like that.

Games and contests create and maintain an atmosphere that provokes people into wanting to do their personal best. And customers can feel that.

Games and contests create bursts of energy that cause people to do extraordinary things. And when people start doing extraordinary things—and are recognized for it— it's fun! It's exciting! And it produces dramatic results.

I know you'll find the games that follow incredibly motivating. They'll get your salespeople excited and cause them to do remarkable things. They'll create a competitive environment and new, challenging opportunities. And I'm convinced that when faced with these new and exciting challenges all the time, your people will find some very creative and astonishing ways to increase sales and perform at their personal best.

CHAPTER FIVE
FUN AND GAMES!

We're finally here! It's Showtime. The time for Fun and Games. This is the time for you to shine, to turn the jobs your salespeople see as routine and boring into jobs that are stimulating and challenging.

Early on, I pointed out that selling is a repetitive process, a process that can unconsciously program salespeople into maintaining the status quo. They see their jobs as always staying the same, and they believe nothing will change. Selling the same merchandise day after day is pretty predictable and becomes routine with very few surprises. Routines get people into ruts that dull their senses, stifle their creativity, and turn them into robots. They often lack the drive to make improvements, to want to do better.

And the winners are . . .

Our games and contests will breathe life back into your staff's jobs and bring some fun back into the selling process. Each day will bring new experiences, fun things to do, and bigger and bigger sales increases!

100 Retail Games and Variations that Work
We've developed 100 retail games and variations for you to use in your store. All of them work. They've been tested and used with positive results in all kinds of different retail stores including jewelry, sporting goods, bicycle, apparel, shoe, furniture, electronics, and more. The kind of merchandise you sell shouldn't make any difference. If you have salespeople

who are expected to sell and you have shoppers who are expected to buy, you can run just about every one of these games successfully.

Choose a game that you feel will increase a statistic or improve a selling behavior, one that will be fun for your salespeople and your customers. Then check to see if you need to reshape the game in any way.

Some of our games may have to be modified to fit your particular environment. Maybe the rules or the format will have to bend a little to make the game work. There may be circumstances requiring you to set up some exceptions to the rules. In Chapter 2, "Elements of a Game," we talked about these types of situations. However, by beginning each game with the end in mind, you'll think through what you want to do, what it's going to look like, etc. Doing this will help you detect whether or not anything in the game needs to be varied or adjusted.

Individual and Team Competitions

1. Individual Competitions
In individual competitions, salespeople compete against one another. They go head-to-head on their own. To win, they need to get the most out of their own strengths and at the same time, have the courage to change old habits and substitute new ones to be more successful.

The immediate task is to outperform the other salespeople. Salespeople want to be the best. They want to hold center stage, have the spotlight, and get the applause. These achievements are recognized by everyone as individual efforts and individual accomplishments. Individual competition is highly competitive and very challenging.

While we acknowledge the high degree of intensity in wanting to stand out and be the best—to be the outright winner—we still don't like the idea of only one winner all the time. We like a lot of people to win, even in individual competitions. And although the primary purpose of running games and contests is to increase sales statistics and improve selling behaviors, games should also stimulate morale. If all your contests are set up to reward only one winner, then your top achievers will win most often and run away with all the prizes. This is counterproductive to what you want to achieve. People don't want to come to work every morning thinking they're going to lose. It's not very stimulating.

For example, Go for the Gold! is one of the best games I've ever created. It's what I like to call a *BIG* game—a long-running contest with plenty of chances to win, building up more and more excitement as the game goes on. While this game rewards individual achievements, there still can be many gold medal winners, just as in the Olympic Games. That's because Go for the Gold! has many different events: items per sale, sales per hour, total sales volume, and so on.

There's something about this game that inspires people to want to take home the gold in as many events as they can. In their minds they can hear their rivals chanting the words "Bet you can't!" This is the ultimate challenge. And there's nothing to prevent them from capturing as many gold medals as they can. But we usually have more than one winner in this contest. The thing is, everybody knows they've got a shot at something if they just try to do their very best.

When the games are over and the winners are announced, each is acknowledged separately and individually for being the best and for realizing an outstanding achievement.

2. Team Competitions

It's a lot of fun when you compete against coworkers for recognition. Competing against your friends for recognition and going after the big prize is always an exciting time. There's no doubt in my mind that these feelings become more pronounced when you're part of a team.

I've seen it again and again. When there's a team effort going on, the competitive intensity is even more visible than with individual events.

I've actually seen many salespeople find the energy to take that one extra shot just before their store is ready to close. Why? The peer pressure. They want to make that sale for the team. They don't want to go back and tell their teammates they failed. It's embarrassing. Who wants to think they let down the team? Who wants to be singled out as a non-contributor?

Teams are natural work units. There's a special sense of power and "esprit de corps" in meeting a goal or winning a game in a team competition. I think that's why people love playing on teams so much. They love the camaraderie and the sharing of experiences. There's something special about celebrating successes with others and something very bonding about suffering losses with others, too.

3. Skill Development Games

Games and contests are fun, which makes them an enjoyable way to learn. The skill development games included in our collection don't necessarily produce increases in statistics at the time they're being played. But you do need to run these games to help your people learn.

I've included the skill development games because of their proven success in developing and improving selling skills. Just like the games and contests developed to improve statistics, they boost interest and involvement by stimulating excitement and competition.

In these games, players are given the chance to digest, understand, and absorb new knowledge skills. They then have the opportunity to practice what they've learned in a non-threatening environment. They are given immediate feedback about how they're doing. This is fun and it's such an effective way to prepare salespeople for the real thing—doing it on the selling floor.

Suppose you want to run a game to increase the average items per sale in your store, but your sales staff is having difficulty with add-ons. Playing The Add-on Game might be just the thing they need. Each player gets specific and immediate feedback about his or her performance. You can find out which salespeople need additional training and provide the training. Later on, you can follow up with a contest that rewards people for their average-items-per-sale statistic, and everyone will have a better chance of winning.

In the beginning of this book, I mentioned that while we earnestly believe that salespeople should be dynamic and assertive on the selling floor, we also believe that their behavior should be tied to their customers' expectations. We want the competitive spirit that games and contests create to motivate people to perform at their personal best, day in and day out. We want this competitive atmosphere to help people accomplish extraordinary things. Finally, we want people to enjoy themselves and have some fun.

It is not the intent of this book or of our games to make people aggressive or pushy. No matter how outrageous their desire is to win, your staff's behavior on the selling floor must always be aimed at satisfying your customers' expectations of service.

Managers are responsible for allowing or disallowing certain behaviors on the selling floor. The one thing that you must strictly enforce is your salespeople's seriousness about meeting their customers' needs.

Effective selling skills and outstanding customer service must apply regardless of the game or the contest. You must emphasize that even if losing the contest or the game or the reward at stake, your salespeople are expected to:

Do the right thing for the customer and the future of the company.

Everyone does their best when they're challenged. That's the key ingredient in enjoyable activities such as games. Our collection of games provides this ingredient, which will put some spirit and spark into your workplace.

Let the games begin! Have fun. It's *Showtime!*

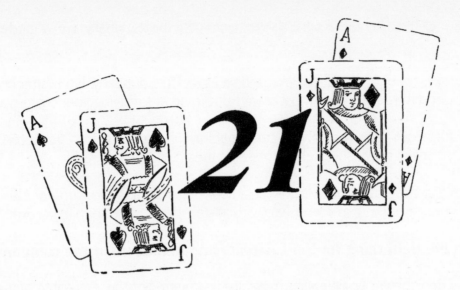

"21"

INDIVIDUAL

This game is used to build sales increases on specific items, such as a new line or new product, a slow-selling item, or promotional merchandise. Sales goals are set for these items, and salespeople who reach a goal earn the right to draw a card. Each salesperson who can hit "21" with his or her cards receives a small prize.

Format　　　　　Individual Competition

Game Play　　　 Set sales goals for the items you want to move. Each time a salesperson achieves one of your goals, he or she draws a playing card from a deck. Salespeople collect cards until they have a combination that totals exactly "21."

Basic Rules

- Each salesperson who achieves a pre-set goal draws a card from the deck.
- Players draw cards until they have a combination that totals exactly "21."
- Each time a salesperson reaches "21," he or she turns those cards in and gets a prize.
- Players hold onto extra cards so they can use them in another hand.
- There's no limit to the number of times someone can get "21."

Suggested Timeframe

One day or weekend

Rewards

Small prizes (see appendix)

Promoting the Game

- Walk your floor and find out what cards salespeople need. Prompt some competition by saying things like, "I'll bet that four you need is the next card up!"
- Enlarge playing-card pictures (ace, jack, king, queen) and use them to decorate the bulletin board in your stockroom, break-room, or office—somewhere very visible to all salespeople.

Props and Supplies

- List of the individual goals needed to draw a card
- Deck of cards
- Prizes

Variations

- Salespeople who draw a natural "21" (a face card and an ace) could win a bonus prize.
- Salesperson who wins the most "21" hands could win a bonus prize.

SAVE THE SALE

INDIVIDUAL

Is your return rate too high? Save the Sale is a great way to encourage your salespeople to turn those returns into exchanges. The best time to run this game is after the Christmas holidays, when return rates are traditionally higher than usual.

Format

Individual Competition

Game Play

Salespeople are awarded points for every exchange transaction: five points for an even exchange; 10 points for a trade-up. If the original salesperson handles a return and cannot change the transaction to an exchange, he or she must give up two points. Salespeople earn rewards based on the Save the Sale points they earn.

Basic Rules

- Salespeople turn in copies of their return and exchange transactions to store management on a daily basis.

- Points are issued by store management upon verification of the transactions.

- Store management keeps a tally board listing the total points earned by each salesperson.

- Customers with returns should be assisted by the original salesperson as often as possible.

- Salespeople choose their own rewards based on the points they earn.

Suggested Timeframe

Three to four weeks, to allow salespeople to accumulate points

Rewards

Set reward levels from small to medium to big (see appendix), based on the number of points earned.

Promoting the Game

- When you announce the game at a store meeting, have your salespeople role-play typical return situations. Discuss items to suggest as alternatives and skills required to make an exchange versus taking a return. Remind your salespeople that return transactions should always be handled in the customers' best interests, regardless of whether a game is running.

- Post a Save-the-Sale tally board in the stockroom, break-room, or office—somewhere visible to all salespeople, to show them their point totals during the contest.

- Display the various prizes in your stockroom, break-room, or office, along with their point values.

- Allow your salespeople a day or so after the end of the contest to select their prizes. You could give each person an order form listing the prizes and their required point values.

- Have an awards ceremony once everyone has selected their prizes. Make it an event to remember.

Props and Supplies

- Tally board
- Prize order forms
- Prizes

UP, UP, AND AWAY

INDIVIDUAL

In this game, every salesperson has an equal chance to win. Salespeople earn the right to pop a balloon by meeting sales goals. Each balloon contains a piece of paper with a prize written on it. The game can be made more exciting by including a variety of prizes and using colorful balloons and streamers.

Format	Individual Competition
Game Play	Various rewards and booby prizes are written on small pieces of paper, folded tightly, and placed inside balloons. Salespeople who achieve designated goals get a chance to pop a balloon and win the prize inside.

Basic Rules	• Post a list of specific sales goals you want your staff to achieve.
	• Each time a salesperson achieves a goal, he or she gets to throw a dart at a balloon to win a prize.
	• If a salesperson pops the balloon, he or she wins the prize listed inside. The balloon must pop in order to win the prize.
	• If the balloon doesn't pop, that's it. There are no second chances.
	• When a balloon is popped, the winner must read the listed prize out loud.
Suggested Timeframe	One day or weekend
Rewards	Use both small and medium prizes (see appendix). If you like, you can even include some booby prizes, such as cleaning duty for the day.
Promoting the Game	• Walk your floor and find out what prizes salespeople need. Prompt some competition by saying things like, "I'll bet that prize you want is in the next balloon!"
	• Take the time to create a colorful game board to hold the balloons. Cover a bulletin or cork board with colored construction or poster paper, and decorate it with streamers. Use multi-colored balloons.
	• Time the game to coincide with someone's birthday, and work the balloons and streamers into a party theme.
Props and Supplies	• Small pieces of paper for recording the prizes
	• Multicolored balloons and streamers for decoration
	• Large cork board or bulletin board that will hold lots of balloons and take the impact of a dart
	• Darts
	• Horns, bells, or whistles to blow when prizes are read

SELL THEM ALL

INDIVIDUAL

Use Sell Them All if you want to move old merchandise or if you want to get salespeople who concentrate in one area to sell a variety of merchandise.

Format	Individual Competition
Game Play	Merchandise is listed on 3 × 5 cards. The cards are spread out on a table, and salespeople must choose a number of cards at random. When salespeople sell an item on one of their cards, they return that card to the manager. The first salesperson to return all of his or her cards wins.
Basic Rules	• Identify items for the game. You might choose older merchandise. Or, if you need to expose salespeople who work in one area to different types of merchandise, use a variety of merchandise.
	• Take a pack of 3 × 5 cards, and list one item on each card. Spread the cards out on a large table.
	• One by one, blindfold each salesperson and have him or her choose 5 to 10 items (determine the number in advance).
	• Salespeople who sell an item listed on one of their cards return that card. The first person to return all of his or her cards wins.
Suggested Timeframe	A weekend
Rewards	Medium prize for the winner (see appendix)

Promoting the Game

- Have fun when choosing the cards. Encourage the other salespeople to egg-on the blindfolded salesperson, telling him or her to not pick or to go for certain cards.

- Keep a running tally of the cards returned by each salesperson.

Props and Supplies

- Index cards

- Tally board

- Prize for the winner

BURIED TREASURE

INDIVIDUAL

Buried Treasure is a theme game that will focus your sales staff on meeting specific sales goals. Each time salespeople meet a goal, they earn a chance to guess where the treasure is buried.

Format	Individual Competition
Game Play	Each time salespeople meet a pre-set sales goal, they earn a chance to guess the location of buried treasure. Colored stickers are used to mark each location on a treasure map. Salespeople try to earn as many guesses as possible.

Basic Rules

- A list of sales goals is determined.

- A large treasure map is posted in a visible location.

- Salespeople are identified by different colors. Each time salespeople achieve a specific sales goal, they use a colored sticker to mark a spot on the map where they think the buried treasure is located.

- The locations of the buried treasure are revealed at the end of the contest. Players who have placed stickers in those locations win prizes.

Suggested Timeframe	A weekend, up to a week
Rewards	Medium prizes for locating buried treasure (see appendix)

Promoting the Game

- Build around a pirate theme. When you announce the contest, wear a bandanna on your head, a patch over one eye, and a big hoop-earring in one ear.

- Play traditional pirate songs or sea shanties when you announce the contest and before store opening and after closing.

- Ring a captain's bell whenever someone meets a goal and places a sticker on the map.

- Post the treasure map on a big bulletin board or wall of your stockroom, break-room, or office. Put it in a visible location to remind everyone that the game is in progress.

- Hold an awards ceremony when you announce the buried treasure locations. Dress up again as a pirate, and have some fun when you announce the winners.

Props and Supplies

- Post a list of sales goals.

- For the treasure map:

  o Use an actual map, or draw your own. Include landmarks that hint at where the buried treasure might be found.

  o On a transparent overlay sheet the size of your treasure map, mark *X*'s to designate the locations of the buried treasure. Write in the prize descriptions next to the *X*'s. (A sheet of Mylar will work well for your overlay sheet.)

  o Colored dot stickers can be found at any office supply store. Assign a different color to each player.

- Select prizes based on the difficulty of the sales goals you set. You can use cash ($5, $10, etc., marked in each location), merchandise, or other awards. Try including a few booby prizes, such as cleaning duty, to add some more fun to the game.

Variation

Award a prize to the salesperson who has the greatest number of colored stickers on the treasure map.

POT O' GOLD

In this game, salespeople earn the chance to win cash and/or prizes for meeting sales goals. Salespeople choose the path they will take to reach the Pot o' Gold, based on how well they perform in specific sales areas.

Format

Individual Competition

Game Play

Salespeople choose from a selection of paths to reach the Pot o' Gold. Each path requires salespeople to meet a number of different sales goals. The first player to reach the end wins the prize(s) found inside the pot.

Basic Rules

- At the beginning of the game, each player chooses his or her path to reach the Pot o' Gold. Each path uses different, specific sales goals to advance players closer to the end (e.g., number of items sold to one customer, a sale over a certain dollar amount, sales of older merchandise, etc.). Once players choose a path, they may not change their minds.

- Each time players meet one of the goals on their paths, they advance one space closer to the Pot. Certain obstacles are set up to move players back one space as well.

- The first person to reach the Pot o' Gold wins the reward(s) inside.

Suggested Timeframe

A weekend, up to a week

Rewards

Fill the Pot o' Gold with coins or cash, or a special medium-to-big prize, depending on the difficulty of the goals you set. You might also offer small prizes (e.g., gold-foil-covered chocolate coins) at certain points along each path to encourage salespeople to keep trying.

Promoting the Game

- Make a colorful game board out of poster board. Use colored construction paper to create your Pot o' Gold, or, better yet, lay the game board flat on a table and place an actual pot in the center. Fill the pot with the prize or cash for the winner.

- Set up a number of different paths to the Pot o' Gold, based on different sales goals. Fill each path with a variety of goals, set at equal intervals, to be achieved during the course of the game. Goals might include: making a sale of $200 to one customer, averaging items per sale for the day of 1.5, or selling five clearance items in one day. Base the difficulty of each goal on previous store averages, and fill each path with an equal number of goals.

- Also create obstacles that will move a player back one space. Include items such as being late to work, taking a customer return, and so forth.

- Have each player make his or her own game piece. Use four-leaf clovers, leprechauns, and so on. Have each player bring in a photo of his or her face and attach it to a game piece.

- Hold the contest around St. Patrick's Day, and decorate the store around this theme.

Props and Supplies

- Game board and Pot o' Gold

- Game pieces

- Cash or prize for the winner

- Small prizes to give to salespeople who meet goals along the way

TREASURE CHEST

This treasure game allows you to target certain items that you want to move. Keys are placed on merchandise throughout the store. Some of the keys fit locks on a treasure chest. Each time players sell an item with a key, they get a chance to unlock the treasure chest and win what's inside.

Format
Individual Competition

Game Play
A treasure chest is secured with a number of padlocks. Players who sell items with a key attached earn a chance to use the key to unlock the treasure chest. Only some of the keys work. Each player who unlocks one of the padlocks wins a portion of what's inside the treasure chest.

Basic Rules

- Treasure, which can be either cash or prizes, is locked inside a case. The case is locked with a minimum of three padlocks.

- Keys are attached to items throughout the store. Only some of the keys fit the padlocks.

- Each time a player sells an item with a key attached, he or she gets to try to unlock the padlocks.

- Players who unlock one of the locks win a share of the treasure. For example, if you use three padlocks, a player who unlocks one of the locks would win one-third of the treasure.

Suggested Timeframe
One day or a weekend

Rewards
Cash or small prizes (see appendix). You might fill the chest with coins for a realistic effect.

Promoting the Game

- Look in hobby or craft shops for a realistic treasure chest.
- Decorate the area around the chest. Use props with a pirate theme (treasure maps, sand, cutouts of ships, etc.).

Props and Supplies

- Treasure chest
- Padlocks and extra keys
- Cash or prizes
- Decorative props

STRUNG ON A LINE

INDIVIDUAL

Strung on a Line is a good game to run on a slow day when you want to pick up more sales. Each time players make a sale, they get to pick from envelopes hung on a clothesline. If they're lucky, they'll choose an envelope that contains a prize. The more sales they make, the better their chances of winning.

Format	Individual Competition
Game Play	Envelopes are hung on a clothesline with clothespins. Each time a salesperson makes a sale, he or she gets to pick an envelope. Only certain envelopes contain prizes, so salespeople who sell more have a better chance of winning prizes.
Basic Rules	• Take a box of envelopes and enclose certificates for prizes or cash in a few of them. Hang the envelopes on a clothesline in your back room, using clothespins.
	• Salespeople get to pick an envelope each time they make a sale. If the envelope contains a prize, they get to keep it.
Suggested Timeframe	One day
Rewards	Small amounts of cash or certificates for small prizes (see appendix)
Promoting the Game	• List the cash amounts or prizes, and post this list in the back room.
	• Keep track of prizes won on a tally board.

Props and Supplies

- Clothesline
- Clothespins
- Envelopes
- Cash or prize certificates
- Prize list and tally board

PASS THE BUCK

Having a sales contest running at all times is essential if you want to maximize your store's sales. Pass the Buck is an easy game to run—you can start it spontaneously with little planning or preparation. Each time a salesperson makes a bigger sale than the one before, he or she gets to take possession of a cash prize. Gaining possession of the money and then having to give it away makes things very competitive. Your salespeople will work to beat each other for the Buck.

Format

Individual Competition

Game Play

At the beginning of the day, the first person to make a sale is awarded the Buck: $10, $20, or whatever amount you choose. He or she has to hand the Buck over to the next salesperson who makes a sale with a larger dollar amount. At the end of the day, the winner is the person who has had the largest sale. He or she gets to keep the Buck.

Basic Rules

- The Buck is passed from salesperson to salesperson as larger and larger sales are made throughout the day.

- If someone makes a really extraordinary sale, one that would be tough for others to top, allow that salesperson to keep the Buck and start a new game with a new Buck.

Suggested Timeframe

One day

Rewards

The prize is the Buck. Make it any denomination you want ($5, $10, $20, etc.). However, you don't have to pass cash. You could Pass the Gift Certificate, Pass a Day Off with Pay, or Pass No Housekeeping Duties. Find something special to use as an incentive with your staff and create your own Buck.

Promoting the Game

- Ask your salespeople to ring a bell every time they Pass the Buck.

- Have your salespeople pin the Buck to their lapels. Explain that this is a way of getting customers involved in helping them keep or win the Buck. Salespeople can explain the game to their customers. There's no telling how much customers will buy just to help a salesperson keep that Buck.

- Use a tally board to keep track of the current sale to beat.

Props and Supplies

- Bell

- The Buck

- Tally board

Variations

- To add variety to the game, pass two Bucks simultaneously, each relating to a different goal—for example, one Buck for largest sale and one Buck for largest number of items in one sale. Make a tally board for each.

- Pass a certificate for something other than money. Choose something that your salespeople will really value (a free lunch, a day off with pay, merchandise, etc.).

SELLING HIGH AND LOW

INDIVIDUAL

This variation adds a little extra excitement to Pass the Buck by including a Penalty Card along with the Buck (the prize card). The winner is the person with the highest gross sales for the day. The person with the lowest gross sales for the day is stuck with the Penalty Card.

Format	Individual Competition
Game Play	At the beginning of the day, the first person to make a sale is awarded the Buck ($10, $20, etc.). Throughout the day, the Buck is handed over to the player with the largest gross sales. In addition, a Penalty Card listing an undesirable task is given to the player with the lowest or no gross sales. The Penalty Card is passed in the same manner as the Buck. At the end of the day, the player with the largest gross sales gets to keep the Buck. The player with the lowest gross sales must complete the chore listed on the Penalty Card.
Basic Rules	• Gross sales for each salesperson are tracked on a tally board. The Buck is passed from salesperson to salesperson as larger and larger gross sales are made throughout the day. The Penalty Card is handed out to the person with the lowest gross sales, either as soon as each player has made one sale or when all but one player has made a sale. The Penalty Card is passed along throughout the day to the salesperson with the lowest gross sales at any given time.
	• At the end of the day, the player with the highest gross sales keeps the Buck. The player with the lowest gross sales keeps the Penalty Card and must perform the task it lists.
Suggested Timeframe	One day

Rewards   The prize is the Buck in any denomination you want ($5, $10, $20, etc.). Or pass a certificate as a prize. Make your Penalty Card something no one wants to have, like trash duty for the entire week.

Promoting the Game   • Have your salespeople pin the Buck and the Penalty Card to their lapels. Explain that this is a way of getting customers involved in helping them win.

                               • Use a tally board to keep track of gross sales.

Props and Supplies   • Penalty Card (make it stand out)

                               • The Buck

                               • Tally board

THE BIG DRAWING

INDIVIDUAL

This contest is designed to increase overall sales. It rewards superior sales efforts, providing an incentive for your salespeople to do their best by giving them chances to win great prizes.

Format	Individual Competition
Game Play	A large game board lists sales goals (sales per hour, items per sale, etc.) and the number of raffle tickets each goal is worth. The game board is also used to record the number of tickets each player earns. Players keep one-half of every ticket. The other half of the ticket goes into a container for the big drawing.
Basic Rules	• Players post the number of tickets they've won on the game board, next to their name.
	• At the drawing, announce each prize before drawing the winning ticket.
	• The winner doesn't have to be present when the drawing takes place. The winning raffle ticket can be posted and the prize claimed at another time.
Suggested Timeframe	A longer duration is probably best for this contest, either over a weekend or a full week. Sunday evening after work is a good time to hold the drawing.
Rewards	Raffle off lots of prizes—big, medium, and small (see appendix).
Promoting the Game	• Display the prizes that will be raffled off so that your salespeople can see and handle them.
	• Make sure everyone knows when the big drawing will be held.
	• Ring a bell or blow a horn, and make an announcement whenever someone achieves a goal and wins a lot of raffle tickets.

Props and Supplies

- Roll of perforated duplicate ticket coupons

- Game board with two lists: specific sales goals and their values, and the names of your salespeople and the number of tickets they've won

- Large, clear container to hold the duplicate raffle tickets for the drawing

Variations

- If the game is going really well and people are going beyond your preset goals, introduce a Grand Prize to be awarded in addition to the smaller prizes. Announcing a new prize midway into the game should boost sales and give your salespeople even more incentive.

- Randomly put gold stars on some of the raffle tickets. Gold-starred tickets are Instant Winners. Instant rewards should be very small: candy bars, special pens or pencils, fancy cookies, and so on. Gold-starred tickets go into the drum for the big drawing, just like the other raffle tickets.

SAVE A DOG

This game is used to sell slow-moving items and liquidate old merchandise. Use it on a day in the middle of the season to get rid of old stock before new items arrive.

Format   Individual Competition

Game Play   Slow-moving items are identified as Dogs. The salesperson who sells the most Dogs by the end of the day is the winner.

Basic Rules

- List the Dog items you want to move.

- Each time a player sells one or more Dogs, they get to save a Dog from the pound.

- At the end of the game, the salesperson who has saved the most Dogs wins.

Suggested Timeframe

One day

Rewards

Use a formula to determine a cash reward, or award a small to medium prize (see appendix).

Promoting the Game

- Give a pep-talk about Dog merchandise when you announce the game. Ask your sales-people to discuss the features, advantages, and customer benefits for each category or item. Prepare your people to treat Dogs with respect.

- One key to promoting this game is tracking results by saving Dogs from the pound.

  - At a dollar store or toy store, buy a quantity of small plastic toy dogs.

  - On a table or flat surface in your stockroom, break-room, or office, create a big outline of a dog pound and place all the toys inside.

  - Create outlines of homes for each salesperson.

  - Each time a Dog is sold, the responsible salesperson gets to save a toy from the pound and place it in his or her home.

Props and Supplies

- List of Dog merchandise

- Small toy dogs, dog pound, and home outlines

- Prizes

Variations

Although dogs are a natural theme for this contest, let the kind of toys you can find determine the theme of the game. You could save cats, or even save endangered wildlife from hunters.

ITEM DU JOUR

Here's another game to use when you want to target a particular item. Sales of the Item of the Day (the Item du Jour) are worth a set amount of points. The more a player sells, the more points earned. Points are redeemed for cash or prizes at the end of the day.

Format

Individual Competition

Game Play

A point system is set up for selling a particular item. A running tally is kept for each salesperson's points throughout the day. At the end of the day, points are redeemed for cash or prizes.

Basic Rules

- Designate an item as the Item du Jour.

- Set up a point system for selling the Item du Jour. For example:

  ○ One item = one point

  ○ Two items = four points

  ○ Three items = eight points

  ○ Four items = sixteen points

- Points are based on total sales. Using the above system, a salesperson who sold two items to one customer would earn four points. If that salesperson sold one item to a customer an hour later, his or her point total would be increased to eight points.

- Make each point level worth a specific cash amount or prize. For example:

  ○ One point = $0.50

- Four points = $1.00
- Eight points = $4.00
- Sixteen points = $8.00

- Keep a running tally of each player's point totals throughout the day. At the end of the day, players redeem their points for cash or prizes.

Suggested Timeframe

One day

Rewards

Cash or small prizes (see appendix)

Promoting the Game

- Post a chart that shows the points earned for selling the Item du Jour and the cash (or prize) value of the point totals. Post a tally board next to this chart, and track each salesperson's point totals throughout the day.

- If you are awarding cash prizes, count out the money for each winner coin by coin and bill by bill, with the entire sales staff watching.

Props and Supplies

- Tally board

- Point/prize chart

- Cash or prizes

MYSTERY PRIZES

Mystery Prizes will encourage your salespeople to go for certain goals repeatedly. The more times they meet one of the goals listed on the game board, the closer they will be to winning the Mystery Prize corresponding to that goal. To make this game successful, create goals that are a bit of a stretch for your salespeople, but that they can still achieve. Also, try to build up a lot of suspense around the Mystery Prizes.

Format	Individual Competition
Game Play	The salesperson who achieves a specific sales goal the most times during the contest wins a Mystery Prize.
Basic Rules	• Create a game board that matches Mystery Prizes to specific sales goals (e.g., sell two items from a specific product line, make a sale totaling over $100, etc.).
	• Each time a salesperson achieves one of the goals, have him or her initial the corresponding box on the game board. You can verify the results with sales slips or invoices.
	• At the end of the contest, the salesperson who achieves a goal the most times wins the Mystery Prize for that goal.
Suggested Timeframe	One day or a weekend
Rewards	Medium rewards for the Mystery Prizes (see appendix)
Promoting the Game	• Use the game board to promote the contest. Write the prizes on the game board and cover them with wrapping paper and the words "Mystery Prize."

- Each time a salesperson meets a Mystery Prize goal, have him or her initial the game board in the corresponding box and then ring a bell or blow a horn.

- Post large question marks on the game board and around the store, stockroom, or break-room. Put streamers and glitter on them as reminders that a contest is in progress.

- Gift-wrap the Mystery Prizes and display them in the stockroom, break-room, or throughout the store.

Props and Supplies

- Game board

- Mystery prizes

Variation

Award a special bonus to the person who achieves the highest number of all the goals combined.

MYSTERY PRIZES GAME BOARD				
SALES GOALS				
#1	#2	#3	#4	#5
Sell any one of _____ with one add-on	Any single sale over $100	Total sales in one hour exceeding $_____	Sell any one of _____ with two add-ons	Beat your highest sale from the previous hour
MYSTERY PRIZE	MYSTERY PRIZE	MYSTERY PRIZE	MYSTERY PRIZE	MYSTERY PRIZE

CLUE!

In this day-long game, salespeople use clues to guess the identity of a mystery object or person. Each time a salesperson meets a specific sales goal, he or she is given a clue. The first person to solve the mystery wins a prize.

Format
Individual Competition

Game Play
Specific sales goals (sell three items to one customer, make a sale over $100, etc.) are identified for salespeople. Each time a salesperson meets a goal, he or she is given a clue about a mystery object or person. The object is to collect enough clues to solve the mystery and win a prize.

Basic Rules	• Sales goals for the day are identified and posted.

- Sales goals for the day are identified and posted.

- A mystery object or person is chosen, and clues about it are written on small slips of paper. Each time a salesperson meets a goal, he or she is given one clue.

- A salesperson must have met at least one goal and received one clue to make a guess at the mystery object.

- This is a secret contest. Salespeople should be discouraged from sharing their clues with each other.

- As soon as someone guesses the mystery object, the prize is awarded. A new game can then begin.

Suggested Timeframe

One day

Rewards

Small to medium rewards (see appendix)

Promoting the Game

- Decorate a container with glitter and colored question marks. Put the clues inside it.

- Track the results of each game on a "Clue Prizes" tally board in your stockroom or office. Post the winner, the mystery object, and the prize or reward.

- Decorate your stockroom and office with Sherlock Holmes hats, pipes, and magnifying glasses.

Props and Supplies

- List of the sales goals

- Clues (see examples below) written on slips of paper

- Tally board

- Prizes

Clue Considerations

- The clues are handed out in random order, and they are not to be shared. You can repeat them with some variation (e.g., "can weigh up to 3,000 pounds" and "very large"). Make clues as detailed or ambiguous as you like.

- Choose the mystery objects and clues around your industry, a promotion, or the time of year.

Clues for George Washington	
1. Elected official	14. A VIP "Father"
2. Honest	15. In the military
3. Fruit trees	16. An Aquarius
4. He was first	17. Forged the Delaware
5. Mt. Rushmore	18. Wore a wig
6. One dollar	19. Inaugurated twice
7. Valley Forge	20. Politician
8. Cut trees	21. Veto power
9. A general	22. Wooden teeth
10. Has a monument	23. Revolutionary War
11. 5 cents	24. Very famous
12. Martha	25. Attended two inaugural balls
13. Crossed the Delaware	

BEAT LAST YEAR

INDIVIDUAL

Do you have record sales days—times when your salespeople despair of meeting, never mind beating, their sales goals based on last year's numbers? Get them to focus on this year's goal by challenging them with progressive incentives.

Format	Individual Competition
Game Play	Salespeople try to beat their sales goals for this year, based on last year's numbers. The better they do, the bigger the award.

Basic Rules

- Each salesperson is assigned a sales goal for his or her fair share of this year's goal. For example, suppose last year's sales on one day totaled $1,200. The goal this year is $1,320, or a 10 percent increase. Each salesperson is assigned an individual goal to meet his or her fair share of $1,320.

  If there are a total of 34 selling hours scheduled for the day, divide $1,320 by 34. You'll get $38.82. Multiply $38.82 by the number of hours each person is scheduled, and you'll get each salesperson's fair-share goal.

- Incentive rewards are paid to those salespeople who meet or surpass their assigned goals. The higher a salesperson goes over goal, the bigger the reward. For example:

  ○ Goal = $5

  ○ Goal + 5% = $10

- Goal + 10% = $15
- Goal + 15% = $20

- Incentive rewards are paid in cash at the end of each salesperson's shift.

Suggested Timeframe

One day or a weekend

Rewards

Cash, based on the amount available and the difficulty of the fair-share goals

Promoting the Game

- Post the individual goals for each salesperson on a tally board in your stockroom, break-room, or office. Update sales results each hour so that salespeople can track their progress.

- Have an awards ceremony at which you verify sales results and pay out the cash prizes. Do this at the end of each shift.

Props and Supplies

- Tally board

- Prizes

Variation

- Award small prizes for good efforts to those salespeople who don't quite make their minimum goals (candy bars, gum, sodas, etc.).

2	3	4	5	6
2-1	4-5	1-66	1-1	2-2

AND THEY'RE OFF!

And They're Off! is a race game. Race games are fun ways to track sales results. When you incorporate props and decorations to support your theme, whether it's horse racing, car racing, or running, you'll keep the energy level high.

Format   Individual Competition

Game Play   Based on their daily sales, salespeople move markers around a race board toward a finish line. Whoever reaches the finish line first is the winner.

Basic Rules

- A race board is set up with a game piece marker for each salesperson. The race course is marked in equal increments to reflect sales ($200 for each increment, or whatever you choose).

- Salespeople move their game pieces closer to the finish line each day, based on their daily sales.

- The winner is the first person who sells the total amount required to reach the finish line.

Suggested Timeframe

A weekend to a week, or longer if necessary

Rewards

A percentage of the total sales necessary to reach the finish line, paid in cash, or a medium prize (see appendix)

Promoting the Game

- Choose a sport to use as a theme (autos, horse racing, etc.) and create a race board around that theme. Place the race board on a table in your stockroom, break-room, or office. Design an appropriate track (straight or oval) and appropriate game pieces (cars, horses, etc.).

- Make certain you attach a photo of each salesperson to one of the game pieces. It's very important to personalize the game. Have people bring in their own photos, or take instant photos at the store.

- Decorate the area surrounding the race board with pennants, flags, and posters of race cars or thoroughbreds—whatever props you can find.

Props and Supplies

- Race board with distances marked in equal dollar amounts to represent daily sales

- Game pieces

- Racing props

- Cash or prize for the winner

Variations

- Rather than using daily sales to move along the race board, set sales goals (e.g., required average items per sale each day, or selling a specific quantity of promotional merchandise) to move one space toward the finish line.

- Create penalties to move people back a space, and bonuses to move people ahead. Use returns, unexcused absences, and so forth as penalties. Bonuses could result from sales of specific slow-moving items, repeat customers, and so on.

LET'S PLAY GOLF

INDIVIDUAL

Use this game to encourage salespeople to meet and exceed their sales goals. Whether you manage a sporting goods store or have golf enthusiasts on your staff, your salespeople will enjoy equating their individual goals with performance on a golf course.

Format	Individual Competition
Game Play	Over a nine- or eighteen-day period, salespeople receive "strokes" when their sales performance is under goal. The salesperson with the fewest "strokes" at the end of the game is the winner.

Basic Rules

- Determine sales goals for each member of your staff over a nine- or eighteen-day period. Each day represents one hole of the golf course.
- Define Par for each hole.
- Par is awarded to a salesperson who makes his or her goal for the day, and additional strokes are awarded per hole, per day, based on each person's sales statistics for that day. For example:
  - **Birdie:** Up to 5% over goal = 1 stroke under Par
  - **Eagle:** 5% to 10% over goal = 2 strokes under Par
  - **Hole-in-One:** Above 10% over goal = 1 stroke
  - **Bogey:** Short of goal by less than 5% = 1 stroke over Par
  - **Double Bogey:** Short of goal by 5% to 10% = 2 strokes over Par
  - **Triple Bogey:** Short of goal by more than 10% = 3 strokes over Par
  - **X-Out Hole:** Absent from work on scheduled day with an invalid excuse = 10 strokes over Par.

Suggested Timeframe

Nine- to eighteen-day work period

Rewards

- Award medium to big prize for the winner with the lowest score.
- Award small prizes during the game to any player who makes a hole-in-one.

Promoting the Game

- Announce the game dressed in an old-time golfing outfit, complete with knickers, knee socks, vest, ascot, and cap. Carry a golf club.
- Mount all the players' scorecards on a wall of the stockroom, break-room, or office.
- Post a comprehensive scorecard to track all players' scores, hole by hole, so they can compare their running scores against each other.

- Set up a small putting green in the stockroom or break-room where salespeople can take turns practicing during their lunch and break times.

- Mount a poster of a local or famous golf course, and have your salespeople chart their progress from hole to hole.

- Run the game during a major PGA championship.

Props and Supplies

- List of the individual goals that represent each hole

- Comprehensive scorecard for all players

- Poster of a real golf course so salespeople can chart their progress

- Putters, golf trays, and golf balls

- Prizes

	Let's Play Golf Comprehensive Scorecard									
Player	**1st Hole**	**2nd Hole**	**3rd Hole**	**4th Hole**	**5th Hole**	**6th Hole**	**7th Hole**	**8th Hole**	**9th Hole**	**Total Score**
Amy	4	3	2	4	2	5	1	4	4	29
Bob	3	4	3	4	2	4	3	1	4	28
Clark	4	3	4	4	3	4	3	2	1	28
Jerry	2	2	3	3	1	4	1	2	2	20
Susan	5	5	4	5	4	5	4	10	4	46

Note: Par = 36.

MINIATURE GOLF

INDIVIDUAL

This is another golf game. Players who meet sales goals earn handicaps for a game of golf. The better a player's sales performance, the more likely he or she will be to win the golf game and the resulting prize.

Format

Individual Competition

Game Play

Players earn handicaps by meeting sales goals. At the end of the game period, a golf game is held in the store, before opening or after closing. The winner receives a prize.

Basic Rules

- Set up a system to award handicaps to salespeople who meet sales goals. For example, salespeople who are 5 percent over their average-items-per-sale goal for the day might have one stroke deducted from their golf game; salespeople who are 10 percent over their items-per-sale goal earn three strokes off their game, and so on. Add strokes to the games of salespeople who are under goal.

- Keep a running count of the handicaps and post them on a tally board.

- The game period will depend on the sales goal you choose. For an items-per-sale game, you might want to handicap players at the end of each day for one week.

- At the end of the game period, play golf before store opening or after closing. Set up golf trays around the store and supervise the players during the game. Give everyone a golf card to track the number of strokes they take for each hole. Players add or subtract the number of strokes earned as a result of their sales performance.

- The player who takes the least strokes to finish the game wins.

Suggested Timeframe	The end of a weeklong sales contest
Rewards	Medium prize for the winner (see appendix)
Promoting the Game	• Use real putters, golf balls, and inexpensive golf trays from a sporting-goods store.
	• Get some golf scoring cards from a local course.
	• Post the handicaps earned by each salesperson on a daily basis.
	• Mark the course with small, numbered flags, and set up the course to make the game difficult. Go around corners, through tight areas, and so on. Have at least nine holes.
Props and Supplies	• Tally board to post handicaps
	• Putters
	• Golf trays
	• Golf balls
	• Small flags to mark the course
	• Cash or prize for the winner
Variation	Hold the game while the store is open. Each time a player makes a certain transaction (e.g., sells a certain item or makes a sale over a certain dollar amount), that player tries to sink the golf ball from a marked tee. Hole-in-one earns small prize.

A CONTEST AT CHRISTMAS

INDIVIDUAL

Holidays are great times to run games or contests, and Christmas is no exception. Put a little competitive holiday spirit into your store's atmosphere by offering your salespeople an extra incentive to achieve.

Format   Individual Competition

Game Play   Each time a salesperson achieves a goal, he or she claims a Christmas ornament that contains a certificate for a prize. The ornaments are used to decorate the store's holiday tree. On Christmas Eve, salespeople open (or smash) their ornaments to claim the prizes they've earned.

Basic Rules

- Develop a list of sales goals to be achieved, or establish a daily goal to earn an ornament. For example, salespeople might be required to sell 10 percent over their daily sales goal to earn an ornament for the day.

- Purchase colored ornaments for your store's holiday tree. Inside each ornament place a folded piece of paper that lists a small to medium prize (see appendix).

- When salespeople meet the required goal, they claim an ornament by tagging it with an initialed sticker. Dot-stickers can be purchased at office supply stores for this purpose. Salespeople decorate the tree with their claimed ornaments.

- On Christmas Eve, the salespeople get to open their ornaments and receive their prizes as listed.

Suggested Timeframe

The weekend or week before Christmas

Rewards

Small to medium prizes (see appendix). Give each salesperson a special shopping bag to collect their ornaments and keep their prizes in until they go home.

Promoting the Game

Place the Christmas tree in the main store as part of the holiday decorations to remind salespeople of the contest in progress.

- On Christmas Eve, dress like Santa (or have someone play Santa for your store) to trade the prize slips for the prizes.

- Celebrate the occasion with a Christmas potluck dinner. If management provides a main course (ham, turkey, or a meat-and-cheese tray with bread for sandwiches), salespeople can bring side dishes, desserts, and beverages. Or have a late-afternoon coffee-and-dessert potluck.

Props and Supplies

- Holiday tree

- Ornaments (It's best to use some kind of unbreakable ball that can be snapped together and pulled apart around a small slip of paper, or even something edible, like a fortune cookie. If you must use glass ornaments, be sure to place them in a paper bag to shatter them, and carefully remove the prize slip from the pieces.)

- Shopping or gift bags for salespeople

- Prizes

NO FUN TO LOSE

INDIVIDUAL

In this game, salespeople try to get rid of tasks that they would rather not do: cleaning windows and display cases, reorganizing the stockroom, or just about any task you can think of. This game challenges your salespeople to meet certain sales goals to get rid of their tasks, because in this game, it's No Fun to Lose.

Format	Individual Competition
Game Play	Salespeople choose unwanted tasks from one container and sales goals from another container. Salespeople who meet their goals get to give back their unwanted tasks. Salespeople who don't meet their goals have to perform the tasks as assigned.
Basic Rules	

- Develop a list of daily sales goals and a list of tasks that need to be done around the store. Make the sales goals difficult enough so that meeting them will be a real stretch (e.g., making a sale of over a certain dollar amount to one customer, selling at least _____ stereos today, etc.). For the unwanted tasks, choose items that can wait a few days to be completed, in the event that your salespeople meet all their goals.

- Have each salesperson choose a goal from one container and an unwanted task from another. Have salespeople post their goals and unwanted tasks on a game board.

- At the end of the day, salespeople who meet their goals get to put their unwanted tasks back into the container. Salespeople who do not meet their goals must complete their assigned tasks within a certain timeframe (24 or 48 hours—set this in advance).

- Repeat the game each day for one week. The salespeople who meet their goals each day (or the salesperson who meets the most goals) win a special prize. Any remaining unwanted tasks are divided up equally among the remaining salespeople.

Suggested Timeframe	One week
Rewards	Medium prizes (see appendix)
Promoting the Game	• Create a game board to display each person's sales goals and unwanted tasks. Have a morning ceremony to draw goals and tasks before store opening, and make an announcement each time salespeople meet their goal and place a task back into the container.
	• Be creative when listing the unwanted tasks on slips of paper. Use colorful paper and markers. If you can, draw pictures of salespeople toiling over their tasks.
Props and Supplies	• Game board
	• Two containers to hold slips of paper
	• Prizes for salespeople who meet the most goals (see appendix)

SALES POKER

Use this game to get your salespeople to beat a statistic, to do better. Goals could include selling over a certain dollar amount, or selling certain items in a particular line. As the game progresses, it's exciting to watch the pot grow. And when you set up the game so that everyone has a chance to win, it's especially fun.

INDIVIDUAL

Format   Individual Competition

Game Play   Each time a player reaches a goal, he or she draws one playing card from a deck. Players continue to add to their hands until the end of the game. The person who can make the best poker hand at the end of the game wins the pot.

Basic Rules	• Develop a list of sales goals.

Basic Rules

- Develop a list of sales goals.
- The game begins with a set quantity of poker chips in the pot. Each time a player draws a card, another chip is thrown into the pot.
- Each time a salesperson achieves a goal, he or she draws a card from the deck.
- The player holding the best poker hand at the end of the game wins the pot.
- When you announce the game, discuss the different poker hands and which hands beat the others.

Suggested Timeframe

One day

Rewards

Assign cash values to the chips in the pot.

Promoting the Game

- On game day, wear a visor, a vest, and garters on your sleeves, like an Old West dealer.
- Before the game starts, shuffle the deck of cards and pin each one face-down on a bulletin board covered with green felt. Each time a salesperson achieves a goal, he or she takes one of these cards off the board.
- Using another deck of cards, design a game board that illustrates possible poker hands and their values.

Props and Supplies

- Decks of cards
- Green felt to cover bulletin board, pushpins
- Pot and poker chips
- Game board

Variations

Award small prizes for various hands, such as one pair, so you'll have more than one winner in the game.

GUESS AND GET

In Guess and Get, salespeople guess the locations of letters that, when spelled out into words, earn them prizes. Players earn one guess each time they meet a sales goal. When salespeople work harder to meet the goal you set, the competition for each prize becomes fiercer. Good prizes and a reasonable goal make for a fun game that will produce good sales results.

Format	Individual Competition
Game Play	Salespeople guess at the location of letters that spell out the names of prizes. Guesses are earned by meeting sales goals. The first player to spell out each prize wins that prize.
Basic Rules	• A list of contest prizes is posted.
	• A specific sales goal that can be met repeatedly over a day or weekend is identified (e.g., selling an item from a specific line; selling three or more items to one customer, etc.).
	• The names of the prizes are spelled out in random locations on a master game board. Each time a salesperson meets the sales goal, he or she gets to guess the location of a letter. The first salesperson to uncover all the letters making up a prize name wins that prize.
	• Salespeople track their progress on individual game boards.
Suggested Timeframe	One day or a weekend
Rewards	Depending on the difficulty of the sales goal you set, choose a small to medium award for each prize.

Promoting the Game

- Make a master Guess and Get game board, and secure it in your office. Create a grid with letters on the X axis and numbers on the Y axis. Spell out each prize in random locations on the grid.

- Give each salesperson an individual game board to track his or her progress. Each game board should have a blank grid the same size as the master grid.

- Each time a salesperson meets the specified goal, allow him or her to take a guess at the location of a prize letter by stating a letter and number from the grid (e.g., F2, E3, etc.). When a salesperson finds a letter (makes a hit), reveal the identity of the letter to that salesperson only. Salespeople should write in each letter they find on their game boards. The first salesperson to spell out an entire word wins the corresponding prize.

- Each time a salesperson makes a hit or wins a prize, blow a whistle or ring a bell. Award the prizes as soon as they are earned, noting the remaining prizes available.

- Decorate a list of the prizes with pictures of each prize.

Props and Supplies

- Master game board and individual game boards

- List of prizes

- Bell or whistle

Variations

Track the number of guesses each salesperson earns on a tally board, and award a special prize to the person who earns the most guesses, regardless of whether he or she hits anything.

POINTS PER TRANSACTION

This is a straightforward game in which salespeople earn points for each transaction they make. Whoever has the most points at the end of the game wins.

Format	Individual Competition
Game Play	Management sets up a point system based on sales performance. Salespeople are awarded a specific number of points for each transaction they make. The winner is the salesperson with the most points at the end of the game.
Basic Rules	• Set up a point system based on the dollar amount of each transaction. In setting up this system, consider your store's average sale and what you'd like people to strive for (see example).
	• Keep a running tally of the points earned by each salesperson.
	• At the end of the game, the salesperson with the most points wins a prize.
Suggested Timeframe	One day or a weekend
Rewards	Medium prize for the winner (see appendix)
Promoting the Game	Post a chart of point values in your break-room, stockroom, or office. Include a picture of the prize to be won by the person with the most points.
Props and Supplies	• Chart of point values
	• Tally board for tracking points earned
	• Prize for the winner

Variation

Make a list of small prizes or cash amounts to be awarded to salespeople who meet specific point levels, in addition to an overall prize for the winner.

POINT SYSTEM	
Transaction of $25–$50	10 Points
Transaction of $51–$100	25 Points
Transaction of $101–$250	50 Points
Transaction of $251–$500	100 Points
Transaction over $500	250 Points

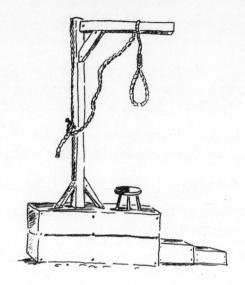

HANGMAN

INDIVIDUAL

This is a good game to use with salespeople who are learning new skills. Salespeople must meet a minimum goal each day of the week to avoid earning a hangman part. Salespeople who have drawn a hangman at the end of the week are assigned cleaning duty or another booby prize. Salespeople without any hangman parts win a prize. By setting reasonable minimum goals (average items per sale, number of customers approached, etc.) for implementing new selling skills, you will encourage your people to apply what they've learned on the selling floor.

Format	Individual Competition
Game Play	The object of the game is to not draw a hangman.

Basic Rules	• Salespeople must meet a minimum sales goal each day to avoid earning a hangman part.

Basic Rules

- Salespeople must meet a minimum sales goal each day to avoid earning a hangman part.

- Each time salespeople don't meet their daily minimum sales goals, they must draw a hangman part on their hangman board. There are six parts in a hangman drawing: (1) the head; (2) the trunk; (3) left arm; (4) right arm; and (5) left leg; (6) right leg.

- Any salespeople who draw a complete hangman at the end of the week receive a booby prize. Salespeople who haven't earned any hangman parts win prizes.

Suggested Timeframe

One day or weekend

Rewards

Minor booby prizes for the losers (cleaning duty, etc.); small to medium rewards for the winners (see appendix)

Promoting the Game

- Post pictures of a hangman's gallows and an empty noose where everyone can see them.

- Play Chopin's "Funeral March" when you announce the game, before store opening, after closing, and during the awards ceremony.

- Plan the game for the week of Halloween, building the theme around witches, goblins, and ghosts.

Props and Supplies

- Picture of a gallows and an empty noose

- Photocopies of the picture with each player's name on one copy

- Prizes

MAKE THE MATCH

INDIVIDUAL

Would you like your salespeople to meet a specific sales goal more than once per day? Are there items that you need to move quickly? Maybe you'd like to see more high-end sales, or more sales from a particular product line. The extra incentive provided by a game and prizes will encourage your sales staff and show them that they are capable of meeting the goals you set.

Format

Individual Competition

Game Play

Salespeople earn vouchers each time they achieve a specific sales goal. Each goal has a different, corresponding voucher. Salespeople redeem their vouchers for cash or prizes. Only two or more of the same vouchers earn cash or a prize. The more times a salesperson meets the same goal during the day, the more matches he or she makes and the larger the cash amount or prize.

Basic Rules

- Make a list of sales goals you'd like your staff to meet more than once each day (e.g., sales over a certain dollar amount, sales from specific product lines, sales of slow-moving items, etc.).

- Players are awarded prize vouchers each time they meet one of the goals. Each goal has a separate, corresponding prize voucher.

- At the end of the day, salespeople redeem their vouchers for cash or prizes.

- Only matching vouchers can be redeemed for prizes. The greater the number of matching vouchers, the larger the prizes. For example:

  ○ Five vouchers, none match = $0

  ○ Two matching vouchers = $0.50

- Three matching vouchers = $1.00

- Four matching vouchers = $2.00

- Five matching vouchers = $4.00

Suggested Timeframe   One day

Rewards

- Cash. Determine your budget prior to establishing the value of different numbers of matching vouchers, and post the values on your prize board.

- Small to medium prizes (see appendix). Pick prizes that you can obtain in multiple quantities, so that salespeople with an equal number of matching vouchers receive equal prizes, or choose several prizes of equal value, so that you have a sufficient number for each level of matching vouchers.

Promoting the Game

- Be creative when making prize vouchers. Use playing cards, and have each suit correspond to a different goal. Or make your own prize vouchers out of colored paper. Have each color correspond to a different goal, and write the corresponding goal on each voucher.

- Make a prize board. List the goals and the prizes for each number of matching vouchers. Enlarge pictures of the prizes or dollar bills, and use them to decorate the prize board. Or display the prizes, and attach the required number of matching vouchers to each.

- Have an awards ceremony at the end of the day. If you're presenting cash, count it out bill by bill and coin by coin.

Props and Supplies

- Prize board

- Vouchers

- Cash or prizes, the size of which depends on the difficulty of each sales goal and the number of matching vouchers required

THE AUCTION

INDIVIDUAL

Salespeople can accomplish extraordinary things when they're working for a prize they really want. In this game, each salesperson makes a personal bet that he or she can increase sales performance by a specific amount. Salespeople who hit their goals are rewarded with prizes they choose for themselves.

Format	Individual Competition
Game Play	In a store meeting, each salesperson bids on raising his or her own sales goal for a specified period of time. Salespeople who meet the new goals name their own prizes.

Basic Rules

- Set sales goals for your staff each week (items per sale, average sale, etc.).

- During a store meeting, salespeople bid on how much of an increase they can produce over and above their assigned sales goals for the duration of the game.

- At the same time, each salesperson chooses the prize or bonus he or she will win upon meeting or surpassing the new goals. For example, Mary may want a specific DVD player if she makes 15 percent over her sales goal, while Jerry may want $100 cash if he makes 10 percent over his goal. You should predetermine limits on bidding for cash and prize options.

- The prizes or bonuses are awarded to those salespeople who meet or exceed their new goals at the end of the contest.

Suggested Timeframe   This works well for a defined promotional period (anniversary sale, back-to-school sale, etc.) that has a built-in timeframe (a week, two weeks, etc.).

Rewards	• Cash. Before the bidding begins, figure out how much you are able to guarantee if your salespeople accomplish what they say they can.
	• Prizes, medium to big (see appendix). Give salespeople options, and let them choose the prizes they want.
Promoting the Game	• Announce the contest at a store meeting. Display current sales goals, and challenge your staff to do better: "How much can you sell? Who can do better than this?" Ask people to set personal goals that represent real accomplishments.
	• Use a dry-erase board or flip chart to keep track of each individual's new goal and the cash amount or prize chosen.
	• After the meeting, post a tally board that reminds your salespeople of two things on a daily basis:
	○ Their sales statistics for each day of the contest
	○ The goals and the prizes they've chosen
	• Paste pictures of the prizes on the tally board to serve as an added reminder.
	• Hold a mini-meeting or make an announcement before store opening each day to remind salespeople about their progress. Encourage them to perform beyond even the goals they've set.
	• At the end of the contest, have a special awards ceremony. Pay cash awards with cash, not checks, and wrap other prizes with big red ribbons and bows.
Props and Supplies	• Sales goals for the time period of the contest
	• Tally board to track each salesperson's progress
	• Cash or prizes

GRAB-BAG

INDIVIDUAL

Grab-Bag is a good contest for non-commission stores. When salespeople meet sales goals, they get to pull a small prize from a grab bag. To give everyone a chance to win, you should make some sales goals easy enough that every salesperson will get to pull a prize at least once. Include some more difficult sales goals, as well, to encourage your salespeople to stretch themselves.

Format   Individual Competition

Game Play   Each time a salesperson achieves a specific goal, he or she chooses a prize from a grab-bag.

Basic Rules

- List the sales goals you want your people to meet.

- Wrap small prizes and place them in a large or oversize bag. Prizes could include small toiletry items, candy, certificates for a free lunch or preferred schedule, lottery tickets, and so forth. Vary the prizes to add excitement to the game. You could even include some booby prizes, such as certificates that assign housekeeping duties.

- Each time a salesperson achieves a goal on the list, he or she selects one wrapped item from the grab-bag.

- Each salesperson wins a grab-bag item only the first time he or she achieves a specific goal from the list. After achieving a goal once, each salesperson must move on to another goal in order to receive another prize.

Suggested Timeframe

One day or a weekend

Rewards

Small prizes (see appendix)

Promoting the Game

- Wrap the gifts creatively—use brown lunch sacks for each gift, and decorate the sacks with stickers and glitter and tie them with yarn or ribbon. Or wrap each gift separately in a special gift-bag or wrapping paper.

- Decorate the grab-bag. Stitch together a couple of old pillowcases and decorate them, or decorate a large canvas tote-bag.

- When you announce the game, show off the grab-bag and some of the wrapped gifts as incentives.

- Ring a bell or blow a horn to announce each time someone reaches into the grab-bag. Make awarding prizes into a ceremony.

Props and Supplies

- List of the individual goals needed to draw a card

- List of sales goals you want achieved

- Large, decorated bag to use as a grab-bag

- Small, wrapped prizes

Variations

- Keep a running count of the number of times each salesperson earns a grab-bag prize. Award a special bonus prize to the person who achieves the most goals.

- Develop different levels of goals—small, medium, and large—and have different grab-bags for each level.

PROMOTE A CATEGORY

This contest can be used to promote a special category of merchandise or to move slow-selling merchandise. You award cash prizes for each item sold from the category you want to move. Create some excitement by asking your vendors to donate a merchandise prize for the overall winner.

Format	Individual Competition
Game Play	Salespeople are awarded "PM" (promotional money/merchandise) for each unit sold from a particular merchandise category. A prize can also be given to the salesperson who sells the most units or records the highest total dollar sales of this merchandise.

Basic Rules

- Designate a promotional category or a category of slow-selling items that you want to move—a new line, a new brand, old merchandise, accessories, and so on.

- Designate a cash amount that will be paid for each unit sold.

Suggested Timeframe   One day, a weekend, or up to a week

Rewards

- Cash

- A medium prize for most units sold or highest-total-dollar sales (see appendix). Try asking the merchandise vendor for a donated prize, or ask to buy the prize at cost (or less).

- There are three ways to handle rewards. No matter which way you present awards, make certain you use *cash*:

  - Pay off your salespeople each day, at the end of their shifts.

○ Hold all payoffs until the end of the game. Reward your salespeople at an awards ceremony. To increase the excitement, count out the PM cash bill by bill. If you give a vendor-donated prize to the overall winner, invite a vendor representative to present the award.

○ Pay your salespeople immediately, after each time they sell an item from the promotional category.

Promoting the Game

• When you announce the game, ask each person to demonstrate an item from the category to the rest of the sales staff.

• Create a promotional category tally board to track sales. You could assign a different color to each salesperson and have them post one sticker, in a corresponding color, on the tally board for each unit they sell. Office supply stores sell colored dot stickers that are good for this purpose. You may want to verify sales using sales slips or invoices. Have your salespeople write the date each sale is made on the stickers to help you check the tally for accuracy.

• Have your salespeople ring a bell or blow a horn to announce each time they sell a unit from the promotional category.

Props and Supplies

• Tally board

• Brightly colored stickers, one color for each salesperson

• Cash, enough for each unit sold

• Prize for most units sold or highest-total-dollar sales

THE MONEY PIN

INDIVIDUAL

In The Money Pin, salespeople compete against each other to earn the right to wear a pin that contains a cash reward. At the end of the contest, a winning time is chosen at random. Whoever was wearing the pin at that time wins the reward. The more often salespeople meet the goal you set, the more often they get to wear the pin and the better their chances of winning the cash inside. The Money Pin can spark intense competition among staff members. Choose your sales goal wisely and you will get good results.

Format   Individual Competition

Game Play   Identify a particular sale that will earn salespeople the right to wear the Money Pin. When a salesperson makes that sale, he or she gets to wear the pin until another salesperson makes the sale. There is no limit to the number of times someone can wear the Money Pin. A winning time is chosen at random, and whoever was wearing the pin at that time wins the cash inside the pin.

Basic Rules

- Management identifies a particular sale as the goal for the game (e.g., selling an item from a particular category, selling ___ items to one customer, etc.).

- The first person to make the specified sale gets to wear the Money Pin. When another salesperson makes that sale, he or she gets to wear the pin. The pin must be worn where it can be seen.

- There is no limit to the number of times a salesperson can wear the pin. Only the minimum set goal is considered. For example, if the goal is to sell three battery packs to one customer, and salesperson A does this, he gets to wear the pin. When salesperson B sells four battery packs to one customer, she takes possession of the pin. If salesperson A then sells three battery packs to another customer, he again takes possession of the pin.

- Salespeople write the exact time they take possession of the pin on a tally board.

- To end the game, the manager picks the winning time at random. The winner is the salesperson who was wearing the pin at that time.

Suggested Timeframe

One day

Rewards

The cash from the Money Pin

Promoting the Game

- Create a Money Pin by purchasing a blank plastic pin from a crafts store and folding a bill ($1, $5, $10, $20) inside. Decorate the pin with rhinestones and beads if you like. Make the pin visible and bold.

- Create a tally board with enough space to list your staff members' names and the times when they were wearing the pin. Decorate the board with photocopies of dollar bills and so on. Post it somewhere visible to all salespeople, such as your stockroom, break-room, or office.

- Have your salespeople blow a whistle or ring a bell to announce when they earn the right to wear the pin.

- Write random times on small slips of paper and put them in a container for the drawing at the end of the day. Make a ceremony of choosing the winning time. You could even have a salesperson do this.

Props and Supplies

- Money Pin containing a cash prize

- Decorated tally board

- Times written on slips of paper

- Container to hold paper slips

Variations

Rather than drawing a specific time, award the prize to the person who had the pin for the greatest total amount of time. Or present two awards—one for the winning time, and one for wearing the pin for the greatest amount of time.

BINGO!

BINGO! provides opportunities for everyone to win. You can be creative by varying the sales goals listed on the game card. Make the game more competitive by posting the BINGO! cards on the wall where everyone can see them. For a different kind of game, place the BINGO! letters on merchandise throughout the store (see variations).

Format   Individual Competition

Game Play   Each salesperson gets his or her own BINGO! card. When players meet one of the goals listed on the card, they earn the corresponding square. Each salesperson who completes a row—vertically, horizontally, or diagonally—wins a prize.

Basic Rules
- Have each salesperson write his or her name on a BINGO! card.

- A salesperson earns a particular square by meeting the goal in that square.

- A player gets BINGO! and wins a prize when he or she completes a row vertically, horizontally, or diagonally.

- Salespeople are eligible to win as many prizes as they can with each card. They must complete an entire card prior to getting another one.

Suggested Timeframe

A weekend or one week

Rewards

Small to medium prizes for earning BINGO! (see appendix)

Promoting the Game
- Mount the BINGO! cards on a wall or bulletin board so that salespeople can see how their competitors are doing.

- When someone gets BINGO!, have that person ring a bell or blow a horn.

- Award prizes on the spot the moment someone rings the bell to announce BINGO! Make a ceremony of awarding prizes.

Props and Supplies
- BINGO! cards

- Prizes

Variations

- Each day, announce the direction that people must attempt to fill in the BINGO! lines—vertically, horizontally, or diagonally.

- Call out a BINGO! letter for each day the game is played (B for the first day, I for the second day, N for the third day, etc.). Salespeople should attempt to meet only the sales goals underneath each day's letter.

- Create your own BINGO! card using your store name.

- Choose different cash amounts as prizes for filling in different lines on the BINGO! card.

- Place tags with each BINGO! card location (e.g., B5, I3) on merchandise throughout the store. When a salesperson sells a tagged item, he or she keeps the tag. At the end of the week, call out BINGO! card locations at random (write them on slips of paper and draw them out of a container). Players who have a tag for each location called out earn the corresponding space. The first player to get BINGO! wins a prize.

SABOTAGE

INDIVIDUAL

If you want to see some strong competition, try Sabotage. In this game, players use sales to sabotage their opponents and win the game. Sabotage will be a faster game for low-ticket-item stores. In high-ticket-item stores, the game will run longer.

Format	Individual Competition
Game Play	Transactions earn salespeople the right to place an *X* over another player's name on a tally board. When a salesperson has a certain number of *X*'s over his or her name, that salesperson is out of the game. The object is to put the other players out of the game before they are able to sabotage you.

Basic Rules

- A tally board is divided into a number of squares equal to the number of players. Each player's name is written in one square.

- Each transaction earns a salesperson the right to place an *X* over another player's name on the tally board.

- Players who have a certain number of *X*'s over their name are out of the game. Choose this number based on your merchandise. If you sell lower-ticket items, make the number higher. If you sell higher-ticket items, make the number lower. The last player left standing wins.

Suggested Timeframe	One day to a weekend
Rewards	Small to medium prize for the winner (see appendix)

Promoting the Game

- Decorate the tally board with cutouts of soldiers, war planes, and so forth.
- Instead of marking *X*'s with a pen, use game pieces, such as cut-out pictures of bombs or missiles.

Props and Supplies

- Tally board (and game pieces, if desired)
- Prize for the winner

LOTTERY TICKET

DATE: _____ PLAYER: _____

1	2	3	4	5	6	7	8	9	10
11	12	13	14	15	16	17	18	19	20
21	22	23	24	25	26	27	28	29	30

WIN THE LOTTERY!

INDIVIDUAL

In this retail version of the ever-popular state lottery, salespeople earn a lottery ticket for each goal they meet. The more goals they meet, the more tickets they get and the greater their chances of winning. If no one wins the jackpot one day, the amount is combined with the jackpot for the second day, increasing everyone's motivation to do well.

Format	Individual Competition
Game Play	Each time a salesperson meets a goal, he or she receives a lottery ticket. Salespeople circle one number on each ticket they earn. At the end of the day, the winning lottery number is drawn, and whoever has circled that number wins the jackpot.

Basic Rules

- Every time a salesperson meets a preset sales goal, he or she receives a lottery ticket.

- Players circle one number on each lottery ticket they earn.

- A winning lottery number is drawn for each day. The jackpot is awarded to the salesperson who has circled the winning number on one of his or her tickets.

- If there is more than one winning ticket, the players split the jackpot.

- Each lottery ticket must be dated. Lottery tickets can be used only on the date they are earned.

- If no one wins the jackpot one day, it rolls over to be added to the next day's jackpot.

Suggested Timeframe

One day, a weekend, up to a week

Rewards

The jackpot could be either cash or a medium prize (see appendix). Be sure you have enough to award to more than one player if the jackpot has to be split.

Promoting the Game

- Use bells, whistles, horns, gongs, or bullhorns to generate excitement and enthusiasm.

- Designate a certain time of day when you'll draw the winning lottery number. Make a big production or ceremony of drawing the winning number. Use a spinning drum with numbered balls if you can, but even a clear container or fishbowl with numbers written on small pieces of paper will work well.

- Create a lottery results board on a wall or bulletin board in your stockroom, breakroom, or office. Post each day's winning number, the winner's name (if any), and the jackpot.

Props and Supplies

- Lottery tickets
- Drum or container from which to pull winning lottery numbers
- Jackpot and/or prizes
- Lottery results board

Variations

Run the game for a longer period of time (perhaps a month), and require salespeople to achieve their daily sales goals to earn a lottery ticket. Pull a winning lottery number only once or twice each week. Award bigger jackpots.

PROFITMAKERS

INDIVIDUAL

Profitmakers is a game designed for stores with sales personnel who are authorized to discount prices on merchandise. The object of the game is to sell the most items at 100 percent retail, increasing the profitability of the store.

Format

Individual Competition

Game Play

Management tracks daily sales and percent to retail. At the end of the game, the player with the most transactions at the highest percent to retail wins.

Basic Rules

- Use sales slips or invoices to track daily sales. Each day, multiply each salesperson's number of transactions by their percent to retail (e.g., three transactions at 90% retail = 270; four transactions at 85% retail = 340). To simplify the game, round off the percentages to even numbers. Add each salesperson's figures for a daily total, and post those totals on a tally board.

- *Note:* Be certain to specify a minimum number of transactions or dollar sales each salesperson must make each day to be eligible to play.

- At the end of the game, take a grand total. The salesperson with the highest score wins.

Suggested Timeframe

One week

Rewards

Medium to big prize for the winner (see appendix)

Promoting the Game

- Before the game, have a discussion at a store meeting about discounting and its effect on the store's profitability.

- Keep a running tally of each salesperson's total score, and post it in the stockroom, break-room, or office.

Props and Supplies

- Tally board

- Prize for the winner

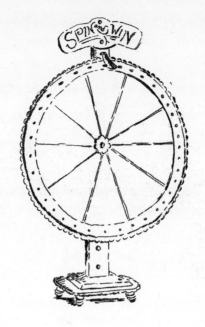

WHEEL OF FORTUNE

In this version of a very popular game, players get a shot at solving a word riddle only after they meet a particular sales goal. The player who solves each riddle spins a Wheel of Fortune for a prize.

Format   Individual Competition

Game Play   Three sales target levels are identified. Each level earns salespeople a different chance to solve word riddles. The first player to solve each riddle spins a Wheel of Fortune for an award.

Basic Rules

- Compile a list of sales goals that can be met over a weekend (e.g., selling ___ items to one customer, making a sale of over ___ dollars). Define three sales target levels for each goal:

    1. Standard (e.g., sell two items to one customer)

    2. Preferred (e.g., sell three items to one customer)

    3. Exceptional (e.g., sell five items to one customer)

- Players who meet a standard sales target are allowed to guess one letter (consonant) of a word riddle. Players who hit a preferred target also are allowed to guess one vowel. Players who meet an exceptional sales target also receive a Free Spin Marker.

- Players who guess consonants or vowels that aren't in a riddle may try to solve it anyway. A player who tries to solve a riddle and fails must hit another sales target before trying again.

- The first player to solve each riddle spins the Wheel of Fortune for a prize. Players who have a Free Spin Marker and are unhappy with their first spin can spin again; however, if they do so, they must abandon the prize from their first spin.

Suggested Timeframe

Weekend

Rewards

Fill the Wheel with small and medium prizes. You might want to use some booby prizes as well.

Promoting the Game

- Display the prizes from the Wheel during the game.

- Post a tally board next to the Wheel, and record each winner and the prize(s) he or she has won.

- Create a colorful Wheel of Fortune and riddle board (see Props and Supplies).

Props and Supplies

- Create a Wheel of Fortune by cutting a circle out of a large poster board. Glue wedges of colored paper inside the Wheel. Write names of prizes or amounts of cash awards in each space. Mount the Wheel on a Lazy Susan with masking tape or Velcro. Set the Wheel on a table, and mark a stopping point to indicate the prizes won.

- Make up a list of word riddles (e.g., names of objects or places, brief phrases, etc.). For each riddle, attach the proper number of self-stick notes to a riddle board made out of poster board.

- Decorate the board. When a player guesses a correct letter, write the letter on the corresponding note(s). Offer clues about each riddle as appropriate.

- Design certificates to use as Free Spin Markers.

- Keep a tally board to list winners and their prizes.

LET'S MAKE A DEAL

INDIVIDUAL

Let's Make a Deal is based on a popular television game show in which contestants who win a prize can trade that prize for another one. The identity of some prizes, however, is concealed. So, a contestant may wind up trading a good prize for a not-so-good one, or a good prize for a better one. In this retail version, the better the salespeople do at meeting their goals, the greater the number of chances they have to make a deal and get a terrific prize.

Format	Individual Competition
Game Play	Salespeople are given a number of chances to make a deal for a prize, based on their sales performance.

Basic Rules

- Set a sales goal for the week for each staff member (e.g., average items per sale, average dollar amount per sale, gross sales, etc.).

- Players record their sales statistics during the week to track their performance against the goal.

- At the end of the week, award chances to make a deal, based on how well each salesperson performs. For example:

  ○ Met goal = one chance

  ○ 1%–5% above goal = two chances

  ○ 6%–10% above goal = three chances

- Make deals with each winner in your office *in private*, while the others wait outside.

- Players choose from prizes concealed in envelopes or inside boxes. After revealing their first prize, players who have earned more than one chance may refuse it and trade it for another. Players do not have to use all of their chances; however, each player must keep his or her final choice.

Suggested Timeframe	One week
Rewards	A variety of small, medium, and big rewards (see appendix), including some booby prizes

Promoting the Game

- During the week, have players record their sales statistics on a tally board that lists their goals. Be sure to list the percentages over goal required to earn more chances to make a deal. Players will be able to track their statistics against the goal and will shoot for as many chances as possible.

- Be creative with your prizes and how you conceal them. You could include different amounts of cash in envelopes, or certificates for prizes *and* booby prizes, like taking out the trash. Inside or underneath boxes, place prizes of varying sizes and values. Use big boxes for little prizes. Include both terrific and not-so-terrific prizes. Make choosing a prize a challenge.

- Have some fun when you make deals. Set time limits for making each choice. Egg-on your salespeople: "Are you sure you wouldn't rather have what's in this nice big box?" After you conceal any revealed prizes, have each salesperson show the others what he or she has won, and invite the next "contestant" in to play.

Props and Supplies

- Tally board for sales performance

- Decorated boxes/envelopes to conceal prizes

- Cash or prizes, varying in size and value (see appendix)

Variation

- Get people who do not meet their sales goals involved so that they'll be motivated to do better next time. Let them be the "audience" for each deal.

SECRET SQUARES

INDIVIDUAL

Use this game when you want to increase sales of a particular item. The more designated items your staff sells, the more Secret Squares they earn. At the end of the game, the value of each Secret Square is revealed.

Format	Individual Competition
Game Play	Each time a player sells an item designated by management as the Secret Square item, that player places his or her initials on one square of a Secret Square game board. At the end of the game, the value of each square is revealed, and the salespeople receive the prizes corresponding to the squares they've earned.
Basic Rules	• Management designates a specific item as the Secret Square item for the game.
	• Each time a player sells a Secret Square item, that player places his or her initials and the transaction number in one square of a Secret Square game board.
	• At the end of the contest, the value of each square is revealed and players receive their prizes.
Suggested Timeframe	A long weekend, up to a week
Rewards	• Cash, in smaller or larger amounts, depending on the sales difficulty of the designated item
	• Small prizes (see appendix)
	• Blank squares, or even some booby prizes, to add extra excitement to the game

Promoting the Game

- When you announce the game, discuss product features for the Secret Square item you choose. Talk about each feature and how to explain the product's advantages and benefits to customers.

- Select your Secret Square item carefully. For a fun, lighthearted game, choose an easy add-on item, so that people can earn lots of squares while they practice adding on. For a more challenging contest, select an item that's harder to sell, but make the prizes bigger as well.

- Make a large grid of squares for your game board and hang it in your stockroom, break-room, or office. This will allow players to compare results. Decorate the area around the game board with question marks, dollar signs, and small boxes tied with bows.

- Cover the game board with a large sheet of clear Mylar and write one prize in the space over each square. When you unroll the Mylar at the end of the game, conduct an elaborate ceremony. Announce the day and time in advance so that everyone can try to attend. (If you can't find Mylar, make a duplicate game board, with the prizes written in each square.)

Props and Supplies

- Secret Square game board and clear Mylar sheet to cover it (or a duplicate game board)

- Secret Square item

- Cash or prizes

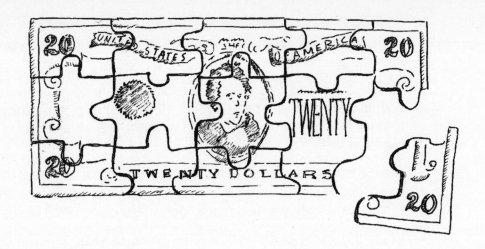

THE PUZZLE GAME

In The Puzzle Game, salespeople earn puzzle pieces by reaching specific sales goals. Players who complete their puzzles win prizes. You can encourage your people to hit an important goal to earn that final piece, whether that goal is a sale with two add-ons or a single sale over a certain amount. The Puzzle Game can be used for a variety of sales goals by changing the timeframe of the game.

Format	Individual Competition
Game Play	Salespeople earn puzzle pieces by meeting specific sales goals. Each salesperson who completes his or her puzzle within the required timeframe wins a prize.

Basic Rules

Enlarge a picture or an item (e.g., a $10 bill) on a photocopier so that it fills an 8½ × 11-inch piece of paper. Draw lines through the picture to represent puzzle pieces. Now copy this onto brightly colored paper. Make one copy per salesperson. Glue or paste each copy firmly onto an 8½ × 11-inch piece of cardboard. Cut each piece of cardboard into puzzle pieces. Keep each puzzle separate, identifying each with a salesperson's name. Give each salesperson a blank 8½ × 11-inch piece of cork board or cardboard to use for assembling his or her puzzle.

- Decide on the sales goals required to earn puzzle pieces and a deadline for completing the puzzles. Give each salesperson a piece of his or her puzzle upon reaching each sales goal.

- Players who complete their puzzle before the game is officially over can begin another puzzle.

Suggested Timeframe

- Difficult goals or lots of puzzles pieces? A weekend

- Easy goals or few puzzle pieces? One day

Rewards

Medium rewards for those who complete puzzles (see appendix)

Promoting the Game

- Keep a running tally of the number of pieces earned by each salesperson, and post it in your office, break-room, or stockroom.

Props and Supplies

- Cardboard, white paper, colored paper, and glue

- Cork board and pushpins that players use to assemble puzzles

- Picture or item to enlarge for puzzle

- Access to a photocopier

SECRET ITEM

INDIVIDUAL

The Secret Item becomes the key to winning in this game. Because salespeople don't know what their Secret Item is, they're challenged to sell everything in the store. Secret Item is a great game to use with promotional merchandise or to move slow-selling items before they're discounted.

Format

Individual Competition

Game Play

A selection of merchandise is assigned point values. Salespeople score points each time they sell one of these items. In addition to regular point value merchandise, certain items are designated as Secret Items. Each salesperson has his or her own Secret Item, and does not know the identity of that item until the end of the game. Secret Item sales are worth extra points. The salesperson with the most points at the end of the game wins.

Basic Rules

- Assign point values to sales of selected merchandise. Choose items you want to move. For example:

    ○ Gift-boxed sports socks = 5 points

    ○ Athletic insoles = 10 points

    ○ Miniature flashlights = 15 points

    ○ Energy bars = 10 points

- Select other items as Secret Items. Write the names of these items on separate pieces of paper and place them in separate, sealed envelopes. Each salesperson selects one envelope and writes his or her name on it. Keep the sealed envelopes in your office until the end of the game.

- Salespeople update a game board each time they make a sale of the regular point value merchandise.

- Salespeople must keep a running tally of all other merchandise they sell. Invoices or sales slips are useful for this purpose.

- At the end of the game, salespeople total their points from the game board and then open their Secret Item envelopes. Each sale of a Secret Item adds extra points to a salesperson's total. For example, each sale of a Secret Item could be worth double the point value of any other item.

Suggested Timeframe   Weekend, up to a week

Rewards   Medium to big prize for the overall winner (see appendix)

Promoting the Game
- Play mysterious theme music (e.g., the music from *The Twilight Zone*) when you announce the contest and every day before store opening and after store closing.

- Post a Secret Item game board on a bulletin board or wall in your stockroom, break-room, or office. Include the list of regular items and their point values, a tally of each salesperson's points to date, and the prize the overall winner will receive.

- Make large question marks of silver glitter on black poster board. Place them strategically throughout the store. Use the same question mark to highlight the Secret Item game board. Put the same question mark on the Secret Item envelopes.

- At the end of the game, make a big production of calculating the final points, opening the Secret Item envelopes, and awarding the prizes.

Props and Supplies
- Secret Item game board

- Secret Item envelopes and slips of paper

- Glitter question marks
- Mysterious music

Special Considerations   Consider this game for seasonal or promotional items, when you have larger inventories. Tie the game into a holiday (e.g., Valentine's Day, Christmas, Halloween).

Variations

- During a long contest, consider having your salespeople choose a new Secret Item each day the game is played. Their Secret Items are revealed each day, and the extra points are added to each salesperson's running total.

- Award extra prizes to:

  - The salesperson who sells the most total items, regardless of point totals

  - The salesperson who sells the most of his or her Secret Item

- Create a chart of prizes to be awarded for various levels of points earned.

MERCHANDISE LIST	
Sell this:	**Earn:**
1 Howdy Doody T-Shirt	5 Points
1 Howdy Doody Belt	9 Points
1 Pair Howdy Doody Shorts	11 Points
Captain Kirk Cologne	13 Points
Captain Kirk Socks and Gloves Set	15 Points
?? Secret Item ??	30 Points

PRIZE LIST	
Earn this many points:	**Win this:**
0 to 100 Points	Housekeeping duties for *X* Days
101 to 250 Points	Lottery Tickets
251 to 500 Points	Box of Candy
501 to 1,000 Points	Extended Employee Discount
1,001 to 1,250 Points	Gift Certificates
Over 1,250 Points	Cash

MONOPOLY

INDIVIDUAL

Monopoly can be easily adapted to a sales environment. In this individual competition, salespeople earn the right to throw the dice and move game pieces around the board for a chance to buy and sell real estate.

Format

Individual Competition

Game Play

Salespeople who meet specific sales goals earn the right to throw the dice and move their game piece around a Monopoly board. The player with the most assets at the end of the game wins.

Basic Rules

- The manager acts as the Banker. Players are given equal amounts of cash to begin with, as directed in the standard Monopoly rules.

- Specific sales earn players a roll of the dice to move around the board. Follow regular game rules in relation to buying and selling properties and Chance and Community Chest cards.

- Players who land in Jail must achieve a specific sales goal *and* pay $200 to get out.

- Play continues until only one player is left, or until the end of the timeframe. Assets are then tallied. The winner is the one with the most properties and cash.

Suggested Timeframe

One day to a weekend

Rewards

Medium prize for the winner (perhaps a Monopoly game) or cash (a percentage of the winner's assets at the end of the game)

Promoting the Game

- Announce the game and pass out initial money dressed as the Banker, wearing an old-fashioned accountant's eye shade.

- Find a very visible place in your stockroom, break-room, or office to place the Monopoly board.

- Post a list of the sales goals to be achieved in order to roll the dice and move a game piece.

- Have salespeople ring a bell each time they achieve a goal, entitling them to roll the dice. Verify sales prior to allowing players to roll the dice. The other players will want to watch when one player moves his or her game piece.

- Create a Jail on the wall near the game. When someone lands in Jail, put his or her name on a card and post it between the "bars." Post a sign with the sales goal to be achieved *plus* the $200 bail to get out.

Props and Supplies

- Monopoly game

- Bell for players to ring

- List of sales goals that must be met to roll dice/get out of Jail

H-O-R-S-E

This game of H-O-R-S-E will make your salespeople focus on achieving a specific goal with their very next sale. It's the ultimate "bet you can't" challenge.

Format

Individual Competition

Game Play

The first salesperson on a list draws a sales goal from a jar. Players who meet their goal on the very next sale pass on the goal to the next player listed. Players who do not meet their goal on their very next sale earn a letter of the word *H-O-R-S-E*, and the next player listed draws a new goal. The challenge continues through the sales staff until only one person remains who has not earned the letters to spell *H-O-R-S-E*.

Basic Rules

- List your salespeople on a piece of paper in random order. Writing their names on pieces of paper and then drawing them out of a hat, one at a time, is the best way to do this.

- Create a list of single-sale goals, such as a sale of at least $25, sale of clearance merchandise, or one sale of two items. Copy these goals onto individual slips of paper, fold them, and place them in a container.

- The first salesperson on the list draws a goal from the container and must achieve it on his or her very next sale. If he or she achieves the goal, the next person on the list must achieve the exact same goal on his or her very next sale, and the challenge continues down the list, player by player, salesperson by salesperson.

- The first salesperson who doesn't achieve the goal earns an *H*. The next person on the list draws a new goal from the container, and that becomes the new challenge.

- Each time a salesperson fails to achieve the goal specified, he or she earns another letter of the word *H-O-R-S-E*.

- The winner is the last salesperson who doesn't complete the word *H-O-R-S-E*.

- A new game can begin when a winner is declared. The game should run all day long.

Suggested Timeframe   One day or a weekend

Rewards   Medium prizes (see appendix)

Promoting the Game
- Create a H-O-R-S-E tally board.

- Ask your salespeople to bring in personal photographs, or take instant pictures of them at the store.

- Cut out the faces and attach them to a picture of a horse.

- Post the horses on the tally board next to the salespeople's names. Each time salespeople earn a letter, they write in the letter next to their picture.

Props and Supplies
- H-O-R-S-E tally board

- Photos of salespeople and pictures of horses

Variations
- Use your store name, or a longer word than *H-O-R-S-E*.

- If any player makes the challenge, but does better than the previous player, then that automatically becomes the new goal. This makes it tougher and more challenging for the next person to succeed.

H-O-R-S-E TALLY BOARD	
Player	**H-O-R-S-E**
Jamie	H __ __ __ __
Jill	H O __ __ __
Brenda	H O R __ __
Curt	H O R S __
Jack	H O R S E

HIDDEN WORDS

INDIVIDUAL

Hidden Words is a traditional puzzle game that you can use to add some fun and competition to your staff's workday. The sample puzzle we've provided is based on selling, but it's not difficult to create your own puzzles to focus on product knowledge for your industry and other topics.

Format	Individual Competition
Game Play	Each time a salesperson meets a sales goal, he or she earns time to solve a Hidden Words puzzle.
Basic Rules	• Each time a sale is made or a goal is achieved, the responsible salesperson earns time to solve the Hidden Words puzzle. For example, you might award 30 seconds for a sale of $25 and a minute for a $50 sale. Use your judgment, depending on your store and its sales volume.
	• At the end of the contest, have your sales staff sit down, all at the same time, and give each person a copy of the same puzzle.
	• Use a stopwatch to give each salesperson the amount of time he or she has earned to complete the puzzle. Salespeople must turn their papers over when their time is up.
	• The winner is the salesperson who finds the most hidden words in the puzzle.
Suggested Timeframe	One day or a weekend
Rewards	Small to medium prizes (see appendix)—perhaps jigsaw puzzles or crossword-puzzle books

Promoting the Game

- Create a tally board to track the amount of time each salesperson earns:

  ○ You might use a dry-erase board for the tally board, or create timecards and hang them next to each salesperson's name on a bulletin board.

  ○ Have salespeople update the tally board when they earn additional time.

- Make a production of timing salespeople when they work on the puzzles. Use a stopwatch and let them know when they have a minute left, 30 seconds left, and so on.

Props and Supplies

- List of goals

- Tally board

- Copy of puzzle for each salesperson (see example)

- Stopwatch (or egg timer) for timing

- Prizes

Variations

- Try developing different puzzles for different themes (salesmanship, product knowledge, etc.). *Hint:* Fill in blank spaces with consonants after you've entered your own hidden words; vowels tend to create words of their own.

- Hold a Hidden Words contest at a store meeting. Give everyone a copy of a puzzle and 10 minutes to complete it. Whoever finds the most words wins a prize.

B	D	H	K	M	P	R	V	X	C	F	J	O	K	N
P	R	S	V	Z	B	D	A	F	H	J	L	B	N	P
S	E	L	L	I	N	G	L	Q	S	V	X	J	Z	C
D	T	G	J	E	L	N	U	Q	S	W	B	E	F	H
Z	A	T	C	L	O	P	E	N	I	N	G	C	W	B
B	I	F	U	A	J	M	Q	T	X	C	G	T	K	N
Z	L	C	S	S	X	D	W	F	V	G	T	I	H	S
C	J	R	T	K	T	Q	Q	L	P	M	B	O	Z	C
X	D	W	O	F	S	B	U	Y	V	G	T	N	C	H
D	T	J	M	S	H	K	E	R	L	Q	M	P	L	N
W	B	D	E	M	O	N	S	T	R	A	T	I	O	N
F	Z	C	R	W	P	D	T	V	F	T	F	S	S	G
V	R	H	Q	J	P	K	I	N	L	M	B	Z	I	C
G	X	D	W	F	P	R	O	B	I	N	G	V	N	G
T	V	H	U	J	T	K	N	S	L	R	M	Q	G	N

B	D	H	K	M	P	R	V	X	C	F	J	O	K	N
P	R	S	V	Z	B	D	A	F	H	J	L	B	N	P
S	E	L	L	I	N	G	L	Q	S	V	X	J	Z	C
D	T	G	J	E	L	N	U	Q	S	W	B	E	F	H
Z	A	T	C	L	O	P	E	N	I	N	G	C	W	B
B	I	F	U	A	J	M	Q	T	X	C	G	T	K	N
Z	L	C	S	S	X	D	W	F	V	G	T	I	H	S
C	J	R	T	K	T	Q	Q	L	P	M	B	O	Z	C
X	D	W	O	F	S	B	U	Y	V	G	T	N	C	H
D	T	J	M	S	H	K	E	R	L	Q	M	P	L	N
W	B	D	E	M	O	N	S	T	R	A	T	I	O	N
F	Z	C	R	W	P	D	T	V	F	T	F	S	S	G
V	R	H	Q	J	P	K	I	N	L	M	B	Z	I	C
G	X	D	W	F	P	R	O	B	I	N	G	V	N	G
T	V	H	U	J	T	K	N	S	L	R	M	Q	G	N

A DAY AT THE RACES

If you want to reward your sales staff with a little fun at the end of a contest, play A Day at the Races. In this game, salespeople are given play money, based on their performance in a sales contest. The play money is used to bet on a "horse race" held in the store. At the end of the race, the play money is exchanged for cash.

Format   Individual Competition

Game Play   Salespeople receive money, based on their performance in a sales contest. The money is used to bet on a horse race in which the progress of each horse is determined by the roll of three dice. At the end of the race, players redeem their play money for cash.

Basic Rules

- Run one of the sales contests in this book and award play money, rather than cash or prizes. A weeklong game is suggested to create anticipation, but you can also use a day or weekend game.
- Hold a horse race at the end of the contest.

  - Use six horses (see Props and Supplies) and three dice.

  - Have salespeople use their play money to place bets on which horse will win the race. One way to do this is to create odds for each horse. For example, if horse #2 has 2:1 odds and horse #6 has 6:1 odds, a player who wins on horse #2 would double his or her money. A player who wins on horse #6 would win six times his or her money.

  - Players take turns rolling the dice. Each roll of the dice determines how far the horses will advance. For example, if three ones are rolled, horse #1 would move three spaces on the track. If two twos and one six are rolled, horse #2 would move two spaces, and horse #6 would move one space. If one five, one four, and one two are rolled, horses #5, #4, and #2 would each move one space.

  - Whoever bet on the horse that finishes first wins play money, based on the amount they bet and the odds for that horse. Play money is then redeemed for cash (determine the conversion rate in advance).

Suggested Timeframe

The end of the last day of a week-long sales contest

Rewards

Cash

Promoting the Game

- Create a racetrack with six lanes, and mark 30 equal increments on each lane. You could simply draw the track on paper, or visit a hobby store if you want to be more creative.
- Use horses from a model or toy store and play money from a board game.
- Mark each player's bet on a flip chart or whiteboard.

Props and Supplies

- Racetrack
- Horses
- Play money
- Dice
- Whiteboard or flip chart

Variation

Play the game repeatedly after any successful sales contest. Designate a certain amount of play money as the sum required to buy a horse. Horse owners split any winnings earned by their horse with the player who bet money on that horse. Allow people to name their horses.

TOUR DE SALES

This game uses the format of a famous international bicycle race, the Tour de France. The Tour de Sales recognizes the best overall performer throughout all the stages of a multiple-day race. The Tour de Sales can spark intense competition. Make it a big production—get everyone involved and use lots of decorations to support the cycling theme.

Format	Individual (or Team) Competition
Game Play	The contest is held over a period of days (stages) with a different goal set for each stage. Points are awarded to the first-, second-, and third-place winners from each stage. Throughout each stage of the race, the overall winner (the player with the highest point total) wears a "winner's badge." At the end of the race, the player with the highest overall point total keeps the winner's badge and wins a prize.
Basic Rules	• Specific goals are identified for each day (stage) of the tour. For example, if the tour were planned for five days, the goals might be:

- Stage One—Flat-Road Race: Highest Average Sales per Hour

- Stage Two—Uphill Climb: Highest Average Items per Sale

- Stage Three—Downhill Speed: Highest Gross Sales

- Stage Four—Flat-Road Race: Highest Average Sales per Hour

- Stage Five—Sprint for the Finish!: Highest Gross Sales

• Points are awarded to the first-, second-, and third-place winners from each stage.

- For example:
  - First place = Five points (best statistic)
  - Second place = Two points (second-best statistic)
  - Third place = One point (third-best statistic)
- Each day of the contest, the salesperson who has the highest point total gets to wear the winner's badge that day. At the end of the race, the player with the highest overall point total keeps the badge and wins a prize.

Suggested Timeframe

Long weekend to a week

Rewards

Medium to big prize for the overall winner (see appendix)

Promoting the Game

- Wear the winner's badge when you announce the contest. Be sure it is attractive and noticeable—something that your salespeople will want to wear. Depending on your store and staff, you might use an attractive piece of jewelry or accessory as the badge and award it as the overall prize at the end.

- Salespeople who earn the badge must wear it. Emphasize its conversational value with customers.

- Hold the race during the actual Tour de France bicycle race. Watch taped or live televised coverage of the event with your salespeople, and discuss how the race is set up.

- At the end of each day, when you announce the first-, second-, and third-place winners, blow a horn or ring a bell, share the results with your staff, and congratulate the overall winner.

- Devise your own game board to track the different stages of the contest:

  - Find a poster-size map to plot a route of the different stages, one for each day of your contest. A terrain map is a good choice.

  - Create a grid below the map to chart each person's progress. Write the stage numbers and the statistics to be measured on the X axis and the name of each salesperson on the Y axis. Have each salesperson enter his or her own statistics, and circle the winning statistics for each stage.

  - Have your salespeople create their own game pieces. Make certain that the game pieces include a photo of each player. You might use pipe-cleaners shaped like bicycles with instant photos of the salespeople glued to them.

- Have the salespeople advance their own game pieces from stage to stage on the map. The pieces should be placed on the board according to who is winning and losing at each stage of the race.

Props and Supplies

- Map of stages and grid to record statistics and advance game pieces

- Game pieces

- Winner's badge and/or prize

Variations

- Use another sport as a framework for the race (auto racing, cross-country skiing, etc.).

- Hold the race as a team game. Select random teams (pairs are a good choice), and use combined average statistics. Salespeople will be even more motivated since they won't want to let their teammates down.

10K

INDIVIDUAL

10K is a highly competitive game. Salespeople try to sell 10 items, in order, as fast as they can. You can use this game to encourage your salespeople to learn all they can about 10 new items, or to improve their add-on skills.

Format

Individual (or Team) Competition

Game Play

Salespeople try to sell 10 items, in order, as quickly as possible. Players record the amount of time it takes to sell each item. The winner is the player with the shortest overall time. You can also award prizes to the player with the shortest time for selling each item.

Basic Rules

- In your stockroom, break-room, or office, display 10 selected items in a row. Identify which item is to be sold first. You can choose new items with features that salespeople should study, or you can choose main items and logical add-ons to improve add-on skills. If you set up the contest as an add-on game, be sure to set up the items in a logical selling sequence.

- Each player must sell the items in the exact sequence presented.

- If an item is sold out of sequence, it doesn't count. However, other items may be sold in between. Each item represents a leg of a 10K race. Players record the time it takes to sell each item. This is not the presentation time to the customer who buys each item, but rather the time spent on the selling floor between sales of each item. For example, it may take a salesperson one hour to sell the first item. A half-hour later, the next two items are sold to one customer. The time for the first leg would be one hour. For the second leg, the time would be 30 minutes.

- The winner is the player with the shortest overall time. You can also award prizes to the players with the shortest times for each leg of the race. If no one sells all the items (finishes the race), declare a false start and find out where the problem is. Run the race again, with fewer items if necessary, or after you have reviewed any required product knowledge or selling skills.

Suggested Timeframe

One day to a weekend

Rewards

Small to medium (see appendix)

Promoting the Game

- Wear running gear and shoes, and use a starting pistol to announce the game.

- Run the game during the Summer Olympics or when a local 10K is being held.

- Track the results on a game board. Take instant photos of the items to be sold. Draw a racecourse on heavy paper or cardboard. Place the photos at 1K markers throughout the course and pin it to a bulletin board in your office, stockroom, or break-room. Create game pieces by gluing photos of the players to cardboard "runners." Advance the figures around the board as items are sold. You can use pushpins to attach the game pieces to the course. Below the running course post the name of each player and the time for each leg of the race.

Props and Supplies

- Ten items set out in exact sequence of how they're to be sold

- Game board with:

  - Pictures of merchandise items

  - Runners made with photos of the players

Variation

Create a relay-race game. Choose teams of two. Have one player sell the first item and then hand the "baton" over to his or her teammate to sell the second. Team members alternate items until all are sold.

ITEMS-PER-SALE PENNANT

INDIVIDUAL

This game can be used to increase sales of items from a particular line and to increase add-on sales. With a baseball theme, the Items-per-Sale Pennant is a fun game to run during baseball season, or at any time of year.

Format
Individual (or Team) Competition

Game Play
A baseball diamond game board is set up to track sales during the game. One merchandise line or category is chosen to promote. A sale of one item from this line earns one base. A sale of one item plus one add-on earns two bases. A sale of one item plus two add-ons earns three bases, and so on. Each day of the game represents one inning, and the player with the greatest number of runs at the end of seven innings (one week) wins the game.

Basic Rules

- A particular line of merchandise is chosen for the game.

- All players start at home plate:

  - Players who sell one item from the chosen merchandise line advance one base.

  - Players who sell one item from the line and one add-on advance two bases.

  - Players who sell one item from the line and two add-ons advance three bases.

  - Players who sell one item from the line and three add-ons hit a home run.

- Each time a player returns to home base, he or she earns one run. Each run is noted on a daily scoreboard with each day representing one inning.

- The winner is the salesperson with the most runs at the end of a seven-day (seven-inning) game. Ties can be broken with extra innings.

Suggested Timeframe

One week. Each day represents one inning, for a seven-inning game.

Rewards

Award a medium to big prize to the overall winner. You could also give small prizes to the winners of each inning (see appendix).

Promoting the Game

- Create a baseball diamond game board. Make it realistic, with a green field, a brown diamond, and base pads. You might use construction-paper cutouts over a cork board.

- Use colored pushpins to represent the players, or, better yet, have players create their own game pieces out of construction paper or pipe-cleaners, and attach a photo of each player to his or her game piece.

- Post a scoreboard near your baseball diamond.

- Run the game to coincide with a baseball championship or the World Series.

Props and Supplies

- Baseball diamond game board

- Scoreboard

- Colored pushpins or game pieces to represent each salesperson

- Prizes

Variation

You can turn this into a team game by assigning players to baseball teams. Players will be encouraged to do their best so they won't let their team down. You could award a team prize (pizza party, etc.).

A WINNING PITCH ON A LOSING ITEM

INDIVIDUAL

I like to believe that there's a customer for every item manufactured and sold. A professional sales-person will find customers for every item in the store, not only for the items he or she happens to like. In this game, you want your staff to make a "Winning Pitch on a Losing Item." You want to prove to them that salespeople don't have to genuinely love something to sell it, and to sell it well. This game will help your people put aside their personal preferences and concentrate on only one thing: satisfying the customer. After all, satisfying the customer is the most important thing, even if it means selling something you personally dislike.

Format	Individual (or Team) Competition
Game Play	Each staff member identifies a Losing Item: their least-favorite item in the store. The winner of the game is the salesperson who has sold the greatest quantity of his or her Losing Item by the end of the game.
Basic Rules	• Schedule a store meeting. A few days in advance, casually ask each of your salespeople to identify his or her least-favorite item in the store. Then, at the meeting, explain how inventory turnover affects the profitability of the store. One at a time, call the salespeople to the front of the room. Ask them to "sell" their Losing Item to another salesperson, who plays the customer. Then announce the game.
	• On a tally board, post each individual's sales of his or her least-liked item only.
	• Tally the number of Losing Items sold by each player at the end of each day and at the end of the game.
	• The person who has sold the greatest quantity of his or her individual Losing Item by the end of the game wins.

Suggested Timeframe	Up to a week
Rewards	Small prizes to the daily winners, a medium prize to the winner at the end of the game (see appendix)

Promoting the Game

- Encourage your salespeople to let everyone know when they sell a Losing Item. They can blow a horn, hum into a kazoo, or ring a bell to announce their success.

- During the game, walk around the sales floor and "talk up" the Losing Items. Accentuate the positive things about them, and how they can benefit customers. Emphasize making a "Winning Pitch on a Losing Item."

Props and Supplies

- Winning Pitch tally board

- Horn, kazoo, or bell

- Prizes

Variations

- Create a list of all the Losing Items and award the prize to the person who sells the greatest total number of items, rather than focusing only on individual Losing Items. This will help to make the game fairer when there are price variations or inherent selling difficulties associated with some of the items. Award small prizes to the players who sell the most of each individual Losing Item.

- Run the contest as a pairs or team competition—which team can sell the most Losing Items?

THE BOWLING GAME

INDIVIDUAL

This is a great contest to reward your salespeople for stretching themselves and improving their daily statistics. The game is easily adaptable from an individual to a team format. Have some fun by offering prizes from a local bowling alley.

Format Individual (or Team) Competition

Game Play This is a 10-day contest. Each day represents a frame. Based on sales performance, players are awarded bowling scores for the day. For example, selling 6 to 10 percent over goal earns a strike, making goal earns a spare, 1 to 5 percent under goal earns nine pins, and so on. The winners are the players with the highest scores at the end of the contest.

Basic Rules
- Define daily sales goals for each salesperson.
- Define the pin values for meeting, exceeding, or failing to meet sales goals. For example:
  - 6%–10% over daily goal = Strike
  - 0%–5% over daily goal = Spare
  - 1%–5% below daily goal = Nine pins
  - 6%–10% below daily goal = Eight pins
  - 11%–15% below daily goal = Seven pins, and so forth
- Post the daily goals and scores for each salesperson.
- At the end of 10 days, the winners are the salespeople with the highest total scores.

Suggested Timeframe

Ten days

Rewards

Small to medium prizes (see appendix)

Promoting the Game

- You could award a small trophy to the big winner, or even make the contest a regular event and establish a rotating plaque award.

- Contact a local bowling alley for prizes like bowling balls, free games, or other discounts.

- Announce the contest wearing a bowling shirt. If possible, have team shirts made for each staff member, and allow them to wear them anytime during the 10-day game, particularly on the final day. (Check local thrift stores for old-fashioned bowling shirts with names embroidered on the front.)

- Find or record audio sound effects from a bowling alley (pins crashing, the ball return, etc.). Play the recording when you announce the contest and each day at store opening and closing.

- Create individual tally cards for each salesperson that resemble bowling score sheets, or get some score sheets from a local alley. Use *X* for strikes and / for spares. List the day's goal on each salesperson's tally card.

- To enhance competition, create a 10-day comprehensive score sheet as a game board to track everyone's running score. Enlarging a score sheet from a bowling alley is a good way to do this.

- Mount the 10-day score sheet on a wall or bulletin board. Decorate it with white-cardboard cutouts of bowling pins.

- Take your staff bowling. Visit a local bowling alley, explain your game, and see if the alley will offer you any kind of promotional incentive. This will also allow you to show your staff how a bowling game is scored.

Props and Supplies

- Individual 10-day bowling score sheets with goals
- Comprehensive 10-day bowling score sheet game board
- Bowling alley sound effects
- Prizes and/or trophies
- Bowling pins and other decorations

Variations

- Make this a team competition. Create teams and have them choose names and colors and wear matching shirts during the contest. The winning team is the one with the highest cumulative score at the end of the game.
- Award a prize or trophy to the salesperson who scores the most strikes during the game.

FIRST IN, FIRST OUT

This contest encourages sales of older, out-of-season merchandise. It's a good game to use between seasons to make room for new merchandise coming in. You can also use it to move items prior to putting them on sale. First In, First Out reminds salespeople that there is a customer for every item. Even merchandise that's been in the store for a while has value, and every salesperson is responsible for selling this merchandise to those customers who will be satisfied by it.

Format

Individual (or Team) Competition

Game Play

The object is to sell old-season merchandise to earn cash or other prizes. Old-season merchandise is identified by different color categories. Sales from each category are worth different commission percentages, cash amounts, or prizes. Players who sell more of the older, "first-in" merchandise earn more money or better prizes.

Basic Rules

- Establish different color categories for old-season merchandise (e.g., green = one year old, red = nine months old, blue = six months old, yellow = three months old). Mark the tickets or tags of the old-season merchandise with colored stickers that correspond to each category. You can find colored dot stickers at most office supply stores.

- Establish a commission percentage, bonus, SPIFF value, or prize level for each color category—the older the merchandise, the higher the amount (e.g., green = 10% commission, red = 7% commission, blue = 5% commission).

- Each time a salesperson sells old-season merchandise, he or she records the color category and amount of the sale on a tally board. Use invoices or sales slips as a check.

Suggested Timeframe	This is a great contest for that last month between seasons, or prior to putting items on sale. The suggested timeframe is anywhere from two weeks to a month.
Rewards	Cash, based on the commission percentage, bonus, or SPIFF on the merchandise sold, or small to medium rewards, based on the categories and amounts sold
Promoting the Game	• When you announce the contest, ask each salesperson to choose an old-season item and demonstrate it to the rest of the staff.
	• Have your salespeople ring a bell or blow a horn each time they sell old-season merchandise.
	• Decorate the tally board with large colored dots and dollar signs ($) or names of prizes.
Props and Supplies	• Colored dot stickers to designate old-season merchandise categories
	• Tally board
Variations	• Award a separate prize to the salesperson who sells the most individual units of old-season merchandise.
	• Turn the contest into a team competition. Award the team that sells the most old-season items a group commission percentage or a cash prize, and let the team decide how to spend the money (pizza party, dinner out, etc.). Or award individual prizes to the winning team members.

COUNT-DOWN

INDIVIDUAL

Count-Down can help you take advantage of selling activity and team spirit already existing in your store at a particular moment. The game also can be used to light a fire under your staff when spirit is lacking. Either way, the results are seen quickly, and everyone has an equal chance to win.

Format	Individual (or Team) Competition
Game Play	• The game begins when you challenge your sales staff to meet a goal within a particular time period. For example:
	○ "Whoever can sell $1,500 between noon and 1 PM wins [a prize]."
	○ "Whoever can sell the most clearance accessories between two and three o'clock wins [a prize]."
	○ "Whoever has the highest average items per sale in the hour before closing wins [a prize]."
Basic Rules	• The game officially starts and ends at a specific time.
	• Each salesperson must record his or her sales statistics on a tally board.
Suggested Timeframe	Short—one, two, or three hours for each challenge
Rewards	Small to medium prize (see appendix)

Promoting the Game	• Focus on sales statistics that your staff needs to work on.

• Ring a bell, blow a horn, beat a drum—announce the beginning and end of each challenge with a flourish.

• Hang a stopwatch around your neck, and remind everyone how much time is left as the game goes on.

Props and Supplies

• Tally board

• Bell, horn, or drum

• Stopwatch

Variation

Turn Count-Down into a team competition by choosing teams of two or three salespeople at random and challenging each team to beat all the other teams on a particular statistic.

TIC-TAC-TOE

This is a retail version of traditional Tic-Tac-Toe. Players earn squares on the Tic-Tac-Toe board by meeting sales goals. You can set up the game as either an individual or team contest. Either way, your store will benefit as salespeople stretch themselves to meet the goals that will earn them Tic-Tac-Toe and a prize.

Format
Individual (or Team) Competition

Game Play
Each time salespeople achieve a preset sales goal, they get to fill in their initials on a Tic-Tac-Toe board. The winner is the salesperson who scores Tic-Tac-Toe with his or her initials first or has the most initials on the board at the end of the game.

Basic Rules

- Develop a list of sales goals you want your staff to achieve (e.g., average sale of over $50 for the day, selling two blouses to one customer, adding on batteries to every sale). Enter each goal on one square of a large Tic-Tac-Toe board. Post the board in your stock-room, break-room, or office where everyone can see it.

- Each time salespeople meet one of the listed sales goals, they put their initials in the corresponding square on the Tic-Tac-Toe board.

- The salesperson who scores Tic-Tac-Toe with his or her initials first wins. If no one scores Tic-Tac-Toe, the salesperson with the most initials on the board at the end of the game wins.

Suggested Timeframe
One day or a weekend

Rewards
Small to medium prizes for scoring Tic-Tac-Toe (see appendix)

Promoting the Game

- Make a big Tic-Tac-Toe board, and post it on a bulletin board or wall in your stockroom, break-room, or office—somewhere that will remind everyone of the game in progress. Have each person use a different colored marker for his or her initials.

- Whenever players achieve a goal, have them ring a bell or blow a horn to alert the rest of the staff that they are about to mark the Tic-Tac-Toe board.

Props and Supplies

- Large Tic-Tac-Toe board

- Colored markers

- List of goals to be achieved

- Prizes

Variations

- Pair up your salespeople in teams. Use a blind selection process: Put everyone's name in a hat, and pull out two names at a time to form two-person teams. Number each team. Put all the team numbers in a hat, and pull out two at a time to designate which teams will compete against one another. Assign each competing team to be either an *X* or an *O* team. Create one Tic-Tac-Toe board per team, and use them the same way as in the individual game. Teams mark their boards with *X*'s and *O*'s as assigned, rather than with their initials.

- Stage a Tic-Tac-Toe tournament. Choose teams and then hold several days or weekends of Tic-Tac-Toe games. Record the number of wins and losses for each team. After each team has played against every other team, hold a championship game between the two best teams and consolation rounds for all other teams. Everyone wins—small prizes for the consolation-round winners, medium to big prizes for the champions (see appendix).

ADD-ON MADNESS

INDIVIDUAL

Add-on Madness is sure to show your sales staff that they can do better at adding on. Salespeople earn points for add-on sales and redeem them at the end of the contest for prizes.

Format
Individual (or Team) Competition

Game Play
Salespeople earn points for each add-on they sell. The more add-ons they sell with each primary item, the more points they earn. Points are redeemed for prizes at the end of the contest.

Basic Rules
- Logical add-ons are defined for primary merchandise items and posted on a game board.

- For example, in a women's apparel shop: Primary Item = Blazer:

    Add-on = Skirt

    Add-on = Pants

    Add-on = Coordinating dress

    Add-on = Coordinating blouse/sweater

    Add-on = Coordinating scarf

    Add-on = Pin for blazer lapel

- In an electronics store: Primary Item = Stereo receiver:

    Add-on = Speakers

    Add-on = CD player

Add-on = DVD player

Add-on = Speaker wire

- The more add-ons sold per primary item, the more points awarded. For example, one add-on might be worth two points, two add-ons worth five points, three add-ons worth 10 points, and so on.

- Salespeople are awarded cash or prizes at the end of the contest, based on their point total.

Suggested Timeframe

A long weekend, up to an entire week

Rewards

Medium prizes (see appendix). Establish a graduated scale of prizes for total points. For example, 200 points gets two tickets to a local theater performance; 400 points gets two tickets to the performance, plus dinner at a nice restaurant, and so forth.

Promoting the Game

- When you announce the contest, ask your salespeople to identify the add-ons for various primary items in your store. Take notes on a dry-erase board or flip chart. Use these notes to develop a game board that lists primary items, corresponding add-ons, and point values.

- Display primary items and logical add-ons in your stockroom, break-room, or office area.

- Have each salesperson track his or her earned points on a tally board.

- Showcase the prizes on or near the tally board or game board.

Props and Supplies

- Game board listing primary items, add-ons, and point values
- Tally board
- Prizes showcased on game board or tally board
- Add-on merchandise display in stockroom, break-room, or office

Variations

- Run the contest as a team competition, allowing team members to combine their accumulated points to earn a team prize or prizes.
- Award a special prize to the salesperson who makes the most add-on sales overall, or to the one who sells the most add-ons in a single sale.
- Assign extra point values for add-on items that are slow sellers.

SCRABBLE

Scrabble is a word game in which salespeople earn letters by meeting sales goals. Salespeople who spell the winning words are awarded prizes. This is a fast-paced game that can be held on a busy Saturday or over a weekend.

Format

Individual (or Team) Competition

Game Play

Salespeople choose a letter at random each time they meet a sales goal. Winning words are posted in advance. The salesperson who spells each word wins a corresponding prize.

Basic Rules

- A specific sales goal that can be met repeatedly over a day or weekend is identified (e.g., selling an item from a specific category, selling over ___ dollars to one customer, etc.).

- Winning words and corresponding prizes are posted. The choice of words should depend on the difficulty of the sales goal to be met. With a difficult sales goal, you might choose a single word. With a sales goal that is not very difficult to meet, you might choose more than one word (e.g., Professional Retail Salesperson).

- Each time a salesperson meets a sales goal, he or she gets to choose a letter at random. Salespeople attempt to spell the winning words on a Scrabble board. Salespeople can intersect another salesperson's word(s) to spell a new word.

- The first person to spell each winning word receives a corresponding prize.

Suggested Timeframe

One day or a weekend

Rewards

Depending on the difficulty of the sales goal you set, choose a small to medium reward for spelling each winning word.

Promoting the Game

- Make a large Scrabble crossword board, and post it in your stockroom, break-room, or office. Use a bulletin board for the background, and create a crossword grid with yarn. Attach the yarn at both ends with pushpins. Decorate the board with large letters, or pictures of your prizes.

- Cut colored construction paper into squares the size of the spaces in the crossword grid. Use a marker to write a letter on each square. Make certain you include enough variety to make the game competitive (e.g., include enough letters to spell the winning words, and add a good number of filler letters that can't be used).

- Place the letters in a large, colorful container. Give salespeople pushpins to attach their letters to the Scrabble board.

- Post a list of your winning words and the prize that corresponds to each.

- Each time a salesperson earns a letter, ring a bell or blow a horn. When a salesperson spells a winning word, award his or her prize immediately, with everyone watching.

Props and Supplies

- Scrabble crossword board

- Pushpins

- List of winning words and corresponding prizes

- Construction-paper letters and container

Variations

- Turn the contest into a team game by choosing teams and allowing teammates to pool letters to form the winning words. Award team prizes.

- In addition to prizes for the winning words, award a special prize to the person who earns the most letters.

FOLLOW THE YELLOW BRICK ROAD

Follow the Yellow Brick Road is what we call a road game. The basic object of a road game is for salespeople to meet specific goals, allowing them to move their game piece from start to finish along a road filled with obstacles. Most road games are built around some kind of theme, and they generally take a lot of preparation. However, you can get a marvelous return on your investment with road games. In this case, two teams compete against each other to reach the Emerald City.

Format	Group Competition
Game Play	Teammates work together to reach the Emerald City before the other team arrives. The Yellow Brick Road is paved with bricks of a particular value, and each time a team's combined sales total the value of a brick, they move forward along the Road. In addition, they may encounter the Wicked Witch of the West (in the form of a return) and lose ground, or reach a green milestone and go Over the Rainbow for a small prize.
Basic Rules	• Divide salespeople into two equal teams.
	• Create a Yellow Brick Road game board. Assign a dollar value to each of the Yellow Bricks.
	• Each team member's sales are recorded on a tally board. As soon as one team's sales add up to the value of the first Yellow Brick, they move their game piece one Yellow Brick closer to the Emerald City. Each team continues to advance, brick by brick, as they reach the required sales levels.
	• Whenever a team reaches a green milestone on the Yellow Brick Road (a Yellow Brick with a green mark or jewel on it), they go Over the Rainbow and choose an envelope containing a certificate for a small prize.

- Whenever a team member gets a return from a sale made during the game, he or she must choose a bad spell (a slip of paper) from the Wicked Witch of the West's Brewing Pot.

- The Wicked Witch's spells could include:

  - Go back one, two, or three bricks.

  - Team must produce twice as much to move to the next Yellow Brick on the Road.

  - The last sale the team recorded doesn't count. Remove it from the tally board.

- The first team to reach the Emerald City wins.

Suggested Timeframe   One to two weeks

Rewards

- Use small team rewards for the Over the Rainbow green milestone prizes (see appendix).

- A team will have accomplished much to reach the Emerald City. The rewards should be medium to big for each team player (see appendix).

Promoting the Game

- Use the built-in theme of *The Wizard of Oz*.

  - Place the Yellow Brick Road game board in a prominent position in your stockroom, break-room, or office where it will be visible to everyone.

  - Ask each team to design a game piece. This could be their favorite *Wizard of Oz* character.

  - Hang a movie poster and pictures from the movie near the game board.

  - Play selections from the movie's soundtrack before store opening and after store closing. Play "We're Off to See the Wizard" when a team advances on the Yellow Brick Road. Play "Over the Rainbow" when a team reaches a green milestone.

- Record the Wicked Witch of the West's cackle (from the movie) to play whenever a player must choose a spell from the Witch's Brewing Pot.

Props and Supplies

- Tally board

- Create a Follow the Yellow Brick Road game board:

  - Mark a spiral of yellow squares on poster board. The center of the spiral is the Emerald City.

  - Assign a value to each Yellow Brick: $100, $200, $300—whatever will work best for your store.

  - Place green marks or glue plastic jewels on certain bricks (e.g., each 10th brick, each 15th brick, each 20th brick, or at random) to create the green milestones.

- Use long strips of different-colored ribbons or paper taped next to each other on a bulletin board or wall to create the Rainbow. Tape different-colored envelopes to the Rainbow for the Over the Rainbow prizes.

- Make up a tally board for tracking sales.

- Find a big black cook-pot for the Wicked Witch of the West's Brewing Pot. Rest a broomstick next to it if you can. Or cut out a pot from black construction paper and mount it on a wall. Place the spells in black envelopes and place them in the pot or mount them on the wall.

Variations

Play Follow the Yellow Brick Road as an individual competition using the same game board. Ask salespeople to make their own game pieces representing their favorite characters from the story.

Road Game Variations

There are many versions of road games. For example:

- *Moonwalk:* By achieving specific sales goals, teams of astronauts earn fuel for a journey from Earth to the Moon. The more they achieve, the faster each team will get to make a moon landing. Prizes can be awarded to the team that lands on the Moon first, and to the salesperson who earns the most fuel for the journey. This promotion can have a space theme. Prizes might include videos of *2001: A Space Odyssey* or Mel Brooks' *Spaceballs.*

- *Pot o' Gold:* There are three or four different routes to the Pot o' Gold. Salespeople may choose the route they want to take depending on what kind of sales statistic they are best at producing or improving. For example, one route could use sales of old-stock merchandise to reach the Pot o' Gold, another could use Items per Sale, and another could use Gross Sales. The first salesperson to reach the Pot o' Gold wins. Gold foil–covered chocolate coins are great as small prizes or featured decorations.

MOONWALK

GROUP

Moonwalk is a team competition in which salespeople earn fuel for their team's journey to the Moon by meeting sales goals. The first team to land on the Moon wins. Special prizes are awarded to the astronauts who earn the most fuel for the winning team.

Format	Group Competition
Game Play	The object of the game is to be the first team of astronauts to land on the Moon. Team members earn fuel for the journey by meeting sales goals. Salespeople can also delay their team by being penalized for returns, and so forth. The team that reaches the Moon first wins a prize, and the salespeople from the winning team who earn the most fuel win additional prizes.
Basic Rules	• The staff is divided into two teams of astronauts.
	• Salespeople who meet certain preset sales goals earn rocket fuel for their team. The more goals that are met by team members, the faster that team will reach the Moon.
	• Malfunctions are identified that will delay a team from reaching the Moon (e.g., arriving late to work, unexcused absences, taking a customer return, etc.).
	• The first team that lands on the Moon wins a team prize or individual prizes.
	• The astronauts who earned the most fuel for the winning team get to take a Moonwalk and win additional prizes.
Suggested Timeframe	A weekend, up to a week

Rewards

Award a medium prize to the winning team or individual prizes to the winning team members. Award small prizes to the astronauts who win Moonwalks (see appendix). Consider prizes with a space theme, such as copies of *2001: A Space Odyssey*, *Spaceballs*, or another space-related movie.

Promoting the Game

- Create a Moon map on a wall of your stockroom, break-room, or office.

  - Cover a bulletin board with black or midnight-blue paper.

  - Create a Sun, Moon, and Earth with construction paper and use aluminum foil for stars.

  - Plot an orbital route to the Moon for two space shuttles.

  - Mark off equal increments on the route to the Moon. Each space represents one gallon of rocket fuel.

- Identify a list of individual sales goals. Each time a salesperson meets a goal, he or she advances the team shuttle one space toward the Moon. Also identify malfunctions, such as arriving late to work or taking a return, that will cause a shuttle to go back one space. Post these lists next to your Moon map.

- Have each team design their own space shuttle and choose a name (*Discovery*, *Endeavor*, etc.). Use construction paper, plastic models, and so on. If possible, place a photo of each team member inside his or her shuttle.

- Keep a running tally of how much fuel each salesperson earns for the team. Post this next to your Moon map.

- When one team reaches the Moon, identify the two or three salespeople who earned the most fuel. These astronauts get to take a Moonwalk. Hold an awards ceremony to recognize the winning team and the Moonwalkers. Play theme music from a related movie or television show (perhaps *Star Trek*).

Props and Supplies

- Tally board
- Moon map
- Space shuttles
- List of sales goals and tally of fuel earnings
- Prizes

GHOST

GROUP

In Ghost, each salesperson is paired with another salesperson to form a team, and their sales results are combined for a team score. The fun thing about this game is that none of the salespeople have any idea who their teammate is, so all of them have to do their very best if they want to win a prize. You may find your staff members achieving extraordinary results on their own, just to be on the winning team.

Format	Group (Pairs) Competition
Game Play	Before the contest begins, each salesperson is secretly teamed with another salesperson (a "ghost"). Salespeople track their daily sales results, and at the end of the game the secret teams are revealed. The winning team is the one with the best combined sales results.

Basic Rules

- Designate secret teams. Write the same number on two slips of paper for each team. Then, mark one envelope per team with corresponding numbers. Fold the slips to conceal the numbers, place them in a container, and have each salesperson draw a number without looking at it. Each salesperson should hand his or her slip of paper back to you. Look at the number on each slip, write the salesperson's name on the slip, and place it into the corresponding envelope. This will create secret pairs.

- Create a Ghost tally board to track each salesperson's daily sales results. You may choose to track items per sale, total sales, or sales from a particular merchandise category, for example. Track the statistic that will measure the area you think your salespeople need to work on or that will measure an area of needed improvement within your store.

- At the end of the contest, open the envelopes and reveal the Ghost teams.

- The team that has the best results at the end of the week or weekend wins.

Suggested Timeframe

One week or a weekend

Rewards

- Give a Ghost prize. Put two medium rewards (see appendix) in a box, and wrap or decorate the box like a ghost.

- Announce a cash award. Put the money in two envelopes held in the hand of a friendly ghost mounted on a wall or bulletin board.

Promoting the Game

- Emphasize a ghostly theme. Announce the contest dressed up as a ghost, and play ghostly music at the announcement and before store opening and after closing. Run the contest around Halloween, when you can decorate the store using lots of appropriate accents.

- Decorate the tally board with ghosts and question marks to heighten the mystery.

Props and Supplies

- Numbered envelopes and slips of paper to designate teams
- Ghost tally board
- Prize

Variation

Include support staff members. Salespeople will realize that they must achieve even more to win, and support staff members will offer help and encouragement to all salespeople, in the event they are part of the winning team.

STORE CHALLENGES

Store Challenges promote a team spirit among your staff. You can also use this type of competition to form a good relationship between your store and another. Compete with another store in your own multi-store chain or with a store located in your mall or shopping center. This kind of competition provides future opportunities for cross- and cooperative selling and is also a lot of fun.

Format	Group Competition
Game Play	One store challenges another store to a contest, based on who can make the best statistics. The losing store performs some kind of service for the winners.
Basic Rules	• Select a store that is similar to yours in size (number of employees, overall sales volume, etc.). Approach the store manager and challenge his or her staff to a competition for a specific time period.
	• Select a category or statistic for measurement, for example, average sales per hour, gross sales for the day or over the weekend, or items per sale.
	• Define the service that the loser will perform. For example, the losing store's staff might have to do a major cleanup at the winning store, or cook dinner for the staff of the winning store.
Suggested Timeframe	A day or a weekend is best for this contest.
Rewards	The prize is the service that's performed by the losing store's staff.

Promoting the Game

- Encourage a real team spirit among your staff members. Remind them of the prize and that you know they all want to be winners, not losers.

- Keep in constant touch with the competing store manager. Announce regular updates on the other store's score and how your store is measuring up.

- Create a game board to track your results and the other store's results.

- Have your staff dress in store colors or get team shirts for everyone to wear during the competition.

Props and Supplies

- Game board to track both stores' results. Post this somewhere very visible to all staff members.

Variation

Split your staff into two teams and run the contest in your own store only.

BATTER UP!

GROUP

Major league sports provide a great format for team competitions, and baseball is certainly no exception. When played during the baseball season, this game can be especially fun. Batter Up! is a great way to build competitive spirit and teamwork among your staff.

Format	Group Competition
Game Play	Each hour is an inning of a baseball game. Two teams score runs based on the combined total sales of their team members during each hour. The winner is the team with the most runs at the end of the game.
Basic Rules	• The staff is divided into two teams.

- Runs are scored based on the combined total sales of team members during each hour. For example, if team members make a total of $400 in sales from 10 to 11 AM, that team scores four runs. If the opposing team had only $200 in sales during the same hour, they would score only two runs. Since each hour represents one inning, runs are posted at the end of each hour.

- If a team member accepts a return of merchandise and cannot turn it into an exchange, his or her team is automatically out and cannot score further runs until the next hour (inning) begins. Or you could deduct a run for each return made.

- Team members post their scores on the game scoreboard every hour.

- A game may last seven or nine innings (hours). Extra innings can be held if the score is tied at the end of the scheduled playing time.

- The team with the highest score at the end of the game wins.

Suggested Timeframe	One day

Rewards

- Winning team members should be awarded medium prizes (see appendix). Baseball-related prizes might be a good idea.

- An MVP (Most Valuable Player) award (a small prize—see appendix) should go to the salesperson on each team whose sales helped score the most runs. You might use game tickets or DVDs of popular baseball movies.

Promoting the Game

- Play "Take Me Out to the Ball Game" when you announce the game and before store opening and after store closing.

- Announce the game dressed in a baseball uniform, especially if there is a local or favorite team. Come in the complete uniform—cap, shirt, sleeves, pants, socks, and cleats—carrying a bat, ball, and glove.

- Encourage your teams to choose names, put up team pennants, and wear team colors (even baseball caps) on the game day, as long as it won't interfere with selling.

Props and Supplies

- Scoreboard
- Prizes
- Baseball music and related props

Variation

Use another major-league sport, such as football or hockey. Be creative with touchdowns and extra points for assists (assisted sales, turning over the sale, etc.).

	1st Inning 10–11 AM	2nd Inning 11 AM–12 PM	3rd Inning 12–1 PM	4th Inning 1–2 PM	5th Inning 2–3 PM	6th Inning 3–4 PM	7th Inning 4–5 PM	Totals
BATTER UP! SCOREBOARD								
Red Sox								
Blackbirds								

TUG OF WAR

GROUP

In retail Tug of War, teammates work together to beat the other team's sales performance. Sales are used to tug the opposing team closer and closer to a mud pit. The prevailing team members win prizes. As with all team games, this contest will promote a healthy, competitive spirit among your sales staff.

Format   Group Competition

Game Play   The sales staff is split into two teams. Each team tries to outperform the other in selling a particular item or merchandise category over a number of days.

Basic Rules

- Split your sales staff into two teams.

- Base the competition on sales of one particular item or merchandise category.

- Use a diagram to chart sales performance for each day of the contest. Using a contest centered on selling DVD players as an example, if the Red team sells a total of five DVD players one day, and the Blue team sells only two, the Red team has a net gain of three DVD players. The Red team gets to tug the Blue team three spaces closer to the mud pit.

- The winning team is the one that performs the best over the greatest number of days and tugs the opposing team over to their own side, through the mud pit.

Suggested Timeframe

A weekend, up to a week

Rewards

Small to medium prizes (see appendix) for the members of the winning team.

Promoting the Game

- Create a Tug of War diagram to chart each team's progress during the game. Post this in your stockroom, break-room, or office where everyone can see it. Divide the diagram into increments, and draw a mud pit in the center. If you can, place photos of the team members on their respective sides of the mud pit.

- Announce team status/performance each morning and evening.

- Encourage the teams to choose names, and allow them to wear team colors during the competition.

Props and Supplies

- Tug of War diagram

- Prizes

Variation

Award a special prize to the player who assists his or her team by making the most sales.

FEED 'EM BEANS!

This team game will build a competitive spirit among your staff to reach certain sales goals. The winning and losing teams go out together for a group dinner. The winners sit down at a deluxe table and are served a luxurious meal of their choice. The losing team sits right next to the winners; however, they eat without a tablecloth, and are served a dull meal—water and beans are good choices. You'll really see the effect this has on your staff when you run the game a second time. No one likes to be treated like a loser.

Format	Group Competition
Game Play	Two teams compete to reach a sales goal (sales per hour, total sales volume, etc.). A tally board is used to keep track of each team's progress throughout the game. It's important that the teams know how they're doing against the competition at all times.
Basic Rules	Make sure your salespeople continuously post their sales figures. This will keep the energy level high and create a very competitive atmosphere.
Suggested Timeframe	One or two weeks
Rewards	The restaurant you choose for the winners' feast could depend on how much is achieved. If the winning team produces outstanding sales, you may want to take them to a nicer restaurant than you originally planned. On the other hand, if the results are not quite as good, you may decide on a more economical location for the meal.

- The Winners:
  - Wear their best clothes
  - Are driven to the restaurant by limousine

- Choose whatever they like from the menu, from appetizers to dessert
- Talk about winning, how they did it, and how it feels to be the winners
- The Losers:
  - Wear their oldest clothes (jeans and T-shirts)
  - Are driven to the restaurant in a pickup truck or beat-up old car
  - Eat beans and water or hamburgers, nothing fancy (they don't even get to look at the menu)
  - Talk about losing and how they could have done things differently
  - May have to pay for the winners' meals (depending on the kind of store you operate and the relationship you have with your people)

Promoting the Game

Collect menus from different restaurants for the players to review. Emphasize that the better the winning team performs, the nicer the restaurant will be.

Props and Supplies

- Tally board listing both teams and their members
- Markers for scoring
- Menus from different restaurants

Special Considerations

Contact the restaurant in advance to discuss the situation. Specify the following:

- The Winners should:
  - Be treated royally by the staff
  - Be personally escorted to their table in full view of the Losers

- Be seated at a beautiful table with a tablecloth, linen napkins, crystal, candles, flowers, and so on.

Explain that the Losers won't be ordering from the menu. Devise a fixed menu, such as hamburgers, hot dogs, beans, or sliced bologna with packaged ketchup or mustard. Whatever the menu is, make sure the meal looks and is dull. The only beverage you should offer is water.

- The Losers should:

  - Arrive at the restaurant first, be ignored, and then told to wait

  - After the Winners arrive, be given directions to find their own table—butted end-to-end with the Winners' table

  - Be seated at a bare table with the most uncomfortable chairs the restaurant can find

  - Receive minimal service

Variations

- The Losing Team cooks dinner for the Winning Team. The Winners develop the menu and the Losers cook it, serve it, clean it up, and pay for it.

- The Losing Team takes the Winning Team out to dinner. Before the game starts, each team selects a restaurant, and the Losing Team chauffeurs the Winners and picks up the check.

TOUCHDOWN!

Touchdown! is football adapted to a retail setting. The object is to score the most points as a team, which is done by making the best sales. This is a terrific game to play during football season and around the Super Bowl at the end of January.

GROUP

Format	Group Competition
Game Play	Both teams have the opportunity to score every hour. Teams are assigned hourly sales goals. When they meet those goals, they score six points. The winning team is the one with the most points at the end of the game.
Basic Rules	• The sales staff is divided into two teams, and hourly sales goals are assigned to each team. Teams that meet their goals score six points. If a team surpasses a goal by a certain amount, they earn an extra point, for a total of seven points.
	• A penalty is assessed against a team that absorbs a merchandise return during play. No points can be scored until the beginning of the next period (the next hour).
	• If a team member makes a single sale that totals the team's hourly sales goal, his or her team scores an automatic Touchdown—seven points—and the end of the period is declared.
	• At the end of each hour, gross sales for all team members are totaled. Scores are posted on the game scoreboard.
	• The highest-scoring team at the end of the game is the winner.
Suggested Timeframe	One day

Rewards	Small to medium team rewards (see appendix)

Rewards   Small to medium team rewards (see appendix)

Promoting the Game

- Decorate the store with football props such as helmets, jerseys, and posters of NFL players.

- Dress as the referee. Wear a black-and-white-striped shirt. Use yellow "penalty flags" and a whistle (with humor) when you give a penalty for a return.

- Have the teams choose names and colors. If possible, allow them to dress in their team colors.

Props and Supplies

- Team scoreboard
- Prizes
- Football props

Variations   Once or twice, blow your whistle and announce a Two-Minute Warning. Any goals achieved before the end of the period are automatically doubled. Do this shortly before the end of a period (it doesn't have to be two minutes).

FOOTBALL SCOREBOARD								
	1st Hour 10–11 AM	2nd Hour 11 AM–12 PM	3rd Hour 12–1 PM	4th Hour 1–2 PM	5th Hour 2–3 PM	6th Hour 3–4 PM	7th Hour 4–5 PM	Totals
Whammos								
Vultures								

SOLD BY THE YARD

GROUP

In this variation on a football theme, teams compete against each other for yardage and points. Sold by the Yard is fun to play and encourages some real competition, since each team charts its progress toward the other team's goal line on a pretend football field.

Format	Group Competition
Game Play	Two teams compete against each other for yardage, field goals, and touchdowns. The team with the highest score at the end of the game is the winner. Also, the individual players who accumulate the most yardage for each team are declared the MVPs—Most Valuable Players.
Basic Rules	

- Develop a list of sales goals and their values in terms of yards, field goals, and touchdowns. For example:

    ○ $50 sale = 5 yards

    ○ $100 sale = 10 yards

    ○ $200 sale = touchdown (7 points)

    ○ Sale of item X = 10 yards

    ○ X + one add-on = 15 yards

    ○ X + two add-ons = field goal (3 points)

    ○ X + three add-ons = touchdown (7 points)

- All players begin on the 50-yard line. Each player moves his or her game piece toward the opposite team's goal line with each individual sales goal achieved.

- Penalties are assessed for individual players as follows: delay of game (arriving late for work or unexcused absence) = 15-yard penalty; illegal motion (paperwork completed improperly) = 5-yard penalty; offside (not following store policies or procedures) = 10-yard penalty.

- Players who earn an instant field goal or touchdown earn points for their team and begin again at the 50-yard line.

- Players score seven points when they gain enough yardage to cross over the opposing team's goal line. They then begin again at the 50-yard line.

- Team scores and individual yardage earned are posted on a football scoreboard.

- The team with the highest score at the end of the game wins. Also, the player from each team who gains the most yardage receives a special award for being the Most Valuable Player.

Suggested Timeframe

One day or a weekend

Rewards

Offer a team reward for the winning team (lunch, dinner, or a movie). For the MVPs, use medium rewards. You might also offer small rewards to each player who earns a touchdown (see appendix).

Promoting the Game

- Decorate the store with football jerseys, posters, and so forth.

- Dress like a referee when you announce the game. Use yellow "penalty" flags and a whistle when you give a penalty to a player.

- Be creative with your football field (use synthetic grass, white chalk, etc.). Have each team choose a name and team color and decorate their end zone accordingly. Use a blackboard or bulletin board to make a realistic scoreboard (see example from Touchdown!).

- Make football-player game pieces out of pipe-cleaners, and attach a photo of a sales-person to each, or let the players make their own game pieces.

- Allow teams to wear their team colors on game days.

Props and Supplies

- Football field

- Game pieces

- Scoreboard

- Football props, whistle, and referee outfit

COMBAT

Combat can have a powerful effect on your salespeople. As members of a battle squadron, teammates share the burden of winning or losing the game, taking "prisoners of war" each time a sales goal is met. Make a full-scale production out of this game, with a model battleground, plastic soldiers, generals, and flags. The excitement will result in sales increases and a more committed sales staff.

Format	Group Competition
Game Play	Two squadrons (teams) engage in Combat. Sales goals are worth a defined number of POWs (prisoners of war). Each time salespeople meet a goal, they get to "capture" the other team's soldiers, or "release" their own soldiers from POW camp. The winning team is the one with the most POWs at the end of the game.
Basic Rules	• Identify sales goals (targets) and list their values in terms of POWs. For example, a sale of at least $50 = three POWs; a sale of at least $75 = four POWs; a sale of certain older merchandise = three POWs. Post the list in your stockroom, break-room, or office.
	• Choose teams (squadrons), or have your salespeople choose them.
	• Each squadron begins with 50 soldiers.
	• Each time salespeople achieve a goal (hit a target), they get to capture the specified number of prisoners and put them in their own squadron's POW camp.
	• Salespeople may release their own team's soldiers from the other squadron's POW camp, rather than taking additional prisoners, if they choose to do so.

- Define when POW captures will occur—after each sale, at the end of each salesperson's shift, or at the end of the day. Playing war games at the end of the day with invoices or sales slips is a good way to run this game.

- A squadron can win in one of two ways:

  - Be the first squadron to capture all the other squadron's soldiers.

  - Be the squadron with the most remaining free soldiers at the end of the game.

  A larger prize or bonus is awarded to a team that captures all the other squadron's soldiers.

Suggested Timeframe   A weekend to a week

Rewards   Medium to big rewards, either for the team as a whole or for the individual team members (see appendix).

Promoting the Game
- Announce the game as "the general." Wear a battle helmet, carry a rifle or some six-shooters (toy-store variety), and wear a string of war medals on the front of a bomber jacket. Drape the wall behind you with an American flag.

- Play "Reveille" at store opening and "Taps" at closing, or play military marches.

- Have each team choose a name. Make team flags, and so on.

Props and Supplies
- For the battleground:

  - Establish your battleground on a table or other flat surface in your stockroom, break-room, or office, near the list of sales goals and their values. Be creative. Use a map of the United States, for example. Use pushpins or colored markers to identify areas belonging to each squadron.

     ○ Create a POW camp at each end and a demilitarized zone in the center.

     ○ Buy plastic army men from a dime store or toy store, 50 for each squadron. You can use different colors to represent each team and/or different quantities of soldiers (green = 10 soldiers; red = 5 soldiers, etc.).

    • Set up the soldiers facing each other on the battleground.

Variations

    • Announce short battles worth extra POWs. For example, announce a battle from opening until noon, in which the squadron with the combined highest gross sales will capture an extra 10 POWs.

    • Identify two specific toy soldiers as generals, who can be captured only by the sale of a particular high-end item or a single large sale (for example, a sale of $1,000 to one customer). Make capturing the other team's general worth a large number of POWs.

    • Write a bonus goal worth extra soldiers on a piece of paper. Place it in the demilitarized zone. Or place a bonus prize in the demilitarized zone that a team member can earn by meeting a specific goal.

    • Encourage teams to make daily challenges. For example, one team might bet 25 soldiers that they can beat the other team on total gross sales for the day. If the other team does not accept the challenge, this would be considered a surrender, and the surrendering team would receive a yellow flag. At the end of the game, the team with the most yellow flags would have housekeeping or some other duty for the entire month.

COMBAT: LIST OF TARGETS	
Targets	**# of POWs Captured**
Sale exceeding $25	1
One add-on	1
Two add-ons	2
One blouse and one skirt	2
Any two leather items	2
Sale exceeding $50	3
One item from X product line	3
Sale exceeding $75	4
Three add-ons	4
Hourly volume exceeding $_____	5

MAKING CONNECTIONS

In Making Connections, teams try to be the first to complete a puzzle and win prizes. Each time a team member meets a sales goal, his or her team earns the right to make connections on a connect-the-dots puzzle. Each player may make a different contribution, but all players will be able to take pride in how they performed together as a team.

Format
Group Competition

Game Play
Teams receive identical connect-the-dots puzzles. When connected, the dots on the puzzles reveal a common object. There are two ways for a team to win prizes: (1) Be the first team to guess the solution or (2) connect the most dots. Each team earns the right to make connections whenever one of its members meets a specific sales goal.

Basic Rules

- Management keeps a copy of the connect-the-dots puzzle for each team.

- Management posts a list of individual sales goals and their values in terms of number of connections earned.

- Each time a player meets a goal, he or she goes to a manager and makes the number of connections earned while the other team members watch. Team members may coach the player making the connections.

- The number of connections earned by each team is posted on a tally board so that each team can measure their progress against the other(s).

- The first team to guess the solution to the puzzle wins a prize. Also, the team that has made the most connections by the time the puzzle is solved (or at the end of the time-frame) wins a prize. If the same team does both, give that team a bonus.

Suggested Timeframe	A weekend, up to a week
Rewards	Use medium rewards for prizes (see appendix).

Promoting the Game

- Create a tally board to measure the progress of each team. Post this in your stockroom, break-room, or office.

- Walk the floor, informing each team of the other teams' progress. Announce whenever a player earns multiple connections.

- Create the puzzle by selecting a picture of a common object. Use tracing paper to draw your dots and numbers, just like in a children's coloring book. Make the puzzle somewhat difficult. The dots can go from the middle to the outside, and then back to the middle again. Some can be very far apart, and others can be close together. Don't give away the picture with the outline you created with your dots. Make one copy of the puzzle on heavy paper for each team.

- Keep the copies separated and locked in your desk. Allow players to look only at their own team's puzzle.

Props and Supplies

- Puzzles

- Tally board

- List of sales goals and corresponding connection values

- Prizes

Variations

Have each player initial his or her connections, and give a reward to the player on each team who makes the most connections.

SELLING AROUND THE WORLD

GROUP

In this game, players move around a map of the world by meeting specific sales goals. The effect of the game can be changed by setting different goals, such as quantities of merchandise from various categories, or higher average sale figures for each leg of the trip. You can make this game a lot of fun by promoting it with posters and brochures from a local travel agency. An oversize map and unusual game pieces will also help.

Format	Group Competition
Game Play	Salespeople move from city to city around the world by meeting sales goals.

Basic Rules

- Salespeople must meet a sales goal (e.g., $500 in one day) to be placed on the map and begin the trip from their home city.

- Salespeople must reach specific, preset sales goals to take each leg of the trip. Using a women's apparel store as an example, the goals might be:

  - Hometown to New York = Sell six sweaters.

  - New York to London = Sell five pairs of pants.

  - London to Paris = Sell two coats.

  - Paris to . . . (and so on, around the world).

- Players cannot skip around the map. Using the above example, a salesperson who sold five pairs of pants would have to wait until he or she sells six sweaters to advance to London. This will encourage salespeople to focus on specific selling skills or product knowledge areas, one goal at a time.

- The winner is the first player who travels around the world and returns to the home city.

Suggested Timeframe

One week or longer

Rewards

- Small prizes for each player when they get to each city (see appendix)

- Medium to big prize for the winner (see appendix)

Promoting the Game

- Use a large, poster-sized world map to plot and track the city-to-city legs of each player's trip. Post this on the wall or on a bulletin board in the stockroom, break-room, or office where everyone can see it.

- Ask a travel agent for posters or brochures for the cities along the way. Display them near your world map.

- Design a special game piece for each salesperson. You could use hot-air balloons, airplanes, or even bicycles if you manage a sporting-goods store or bike shop. Decorate each game piece with the photo of a salesperson. This will personalize the game and make for more competition.

- Ask salespeople who have visited any of the cities on the route to bring in vacation photos and souvenirs from their trips. Have them share these with the rest of the staff.

- Record the music from the movie *Around the World in 80 Days* and play it when you announce the game, each day before store opening, and at store closing.

Props and Supplies

- Large world map for plotting and tracking the route

- Game pieces

- Prizes

- Posters, photos, and souvenirs from cities along the route

Variation

Use other maps (United States, your store's town or state, etc.).

CHAMPIONSHIP SERIES

GROUP

Championship Series is the retail version of a sports playoff series. It is a major contest that requires at least a month to play. Consider holding a Championship Series if you're part of a multiple-store chain. The contest can also be held within a single store with a large staff.

Format	Group Competition
Game Play	The game is similar to football or baseball playoffs. Teams set up within leagues compete against each other for a predetermined time period, and the team with the best score (statistic) wins. The winning teams from each league compete against each other for the league championship. League champions compete for the district championship. District champions compete for the regional championship, and regional champions compete for the company championship. Prizes get progressively larger with each level of achievement.
Basic Rules	• The company is set up into teams, leagues, districts, and regions. Each store could be a team, or stores may have more than one team.
	• A specific sales statistic is selected as the measure of each team's performance (total weekly sales, weekly average sales per hour, weekly average items per sale, etc.).
	• A schedule is set for the "playoffs." First, teams within each league compete. League champions within each district compete for the district championship. District champions within each region compete for the regional championship. Finally, regional champions compete for the company championship.
	• If any teams tie, they compete again to break the tie and the playoff schedule is adjusted accordingly.

Suggested Timeframe	Teams compete over weekends or weeks for a month at each level, or for whatever period of time you choose.
Rewards	Choose progressively bigger prizes for each level of achievement: league champions, district champions, regional champions, and the company champion. You could offer smaller prizes to the second- and third-place winners at each level (see appendix).

Promoting the Game

- Model your championship after a sport (baseball, basketball, hockey, etc.) and use appropriate sporting equipment for decorative props. Make a scoreboard to post team statistics, and post it in your stockroom, break-room, or office. Include the playoff schedule in your display.

- Conduct opening ceremonies for the playoffs and awards ceremonies for the winners. Dress as a referee or coach. Or dress in a player's uniform. Play related music (ballpark music, the National Anthem, etc.). If appropriate, have district or regional managers visit each store to announce the game.

- Have the teams choose team names and colors.

- Schedule the contest during a major league sports championship, and sponsor a store get-together to watch a game.

Props and Supplies

- Scoreboard for statistics, listing the playoff schedule

- Prizes

- Sports props

Variations

- Teams make special bets against their opponents. Challenges are made that one team can beat another by a certain amount, and the loser must do something for the winner (buy lunch, etc.).

- Championship Series can be easily adapted to a single store, as long as there is a sufficient number of staff members to set up teams and leagues. The winning team is the store champion.

ITEMS-PER-SALE CONTEST

GROUP

The Items-per-Sale Contest was originally developed to increase the average items per sale for a multiple-store chain. The game is typically run during an eight-week period. The more successful salespeople are at adding on, the more points they earn toward purchasing items they want out of a contest catalogue. Adapt this game to your own store or chain for successful results.

Format   Group Competition

Game Play   Management sets up a point system to reward salespeople for adding on. At the end of the contest, salespeople redeem their points for prizes.

Basic Rules
- A point system is set up to reward salespeople for their weekly average items-per-sale figures (see example).

- To earn points, a salesperson must sell a minimum total-dollar amount each week, based on the number of hours worked. For example, a salesperson who works 25 hours might have to sell a minimum of $2,500 in order to earn points for the week.

- Bonus points are awarded for outstanding items per sale on any one day. To win bonus points, a salesperson must have worked a minimum number of hours and sold a minimum amount on that day. For example, you might award 500 bonus points for an items-per-sale of 1.75 on one day, provided that the salesperson worked five hours and sold $500.

- Salespeople keep a daily record of their sales results. The sales figures are posted each day, and points are awarded at the end of each week.

- At the end of eight weeks, salespeople redeem their points for prizes.

| **Suggested Timeframe** | Eight weeks is suggested for a multiple-store contest. A single store could run the contest for a shorter period of time. |

Suggested Timeframe

Eight weeks is suggested for a multiple-store contest. A single store could run the contest for a shorter period of time.

Rewards

Offer a selection of prizes based on the number of points earned. Try to get your vendors involved by donating items or selling them to you at cost. Or you could make each point worth a specific amount of cash.

Promoting the Game

- Make a large scoreboard to record the players' statistics each day and the points earned at the end of each week. Post it in your stockroom, break-room, or office.

- If you are awarding prizes other than cash, create a "catalog" of prizes and their point values. Or display the prizes near the scoreboard, and attach a price tag with the corresponding point value written in. With cash, post a schedule of the cash value of points near your scoreboard, and decorate it with photocopies of dollar bills, for instance.

- Build momentum. Point out what the top performers have earned. Ask people what prizes they want to go for. When a person earns bonus points, make an announcement or ring a bell.

Props and Supplies

- Items-per-Sale scoreboard

- Bell or horn to announce major achievements

- Prizes or cash-earnings chart

- Daily sales statistics to track people's sales results (see example)

Variations

If the game is being run among stores in a multiple-store chain, offer the store with the highest point total (based on the store's weekly average items per sale) an all-expenses-paid dinner at a fine restaurant with limousine service to and from the restaurant.

ITEMS-PER-SALE POINT SYSTEM				
Items per Sale for the Week	**Points Earned for Working**			
	5–10 Hours	**11–20 Hours**	**21–30 Hours**	**31–40 Hours**
1.00–1.10	0	0	0	0
1.11–1.20	25	50	75	100
1.21–1.30	75	150	225	300
1.31–1.35	125	250	375	500
1.36–1.40	200	400	600	800
1.41–1.45	300	600	900	1,200
1.46–1.50	425	850	1,275	1,700
1.51–1.55	625	1,250	1,875	2,500
1.56–1.60	875	1,750	2,625	3,500
1.61–1.65	1,250	2,500	3,750	5,000
1.66–1.70	1,750	3,500	5,250	7,000
1.71–1.75	2,500	5,000	7,500	10,000

Note: Items per sale of 1.75 for any day over 5 hours worked with at least $500 in sales that day earns 500 Bonus Points.

GO FOR THE GOLD!

 GROUP

Go for the Gold! is a sales "Olympics," a major contest in which individual competitors go for a Gold Medal in five separate categories. The competition can go on indefinitely, yearly, or quarterly. Go for the Gold! can be played among the sales staff at one store or among the staff members in the chain, region, or district. No matter which way you choose to organize this grand event, make sure to give it the promotion it deserves. The winner of each Gold Medal should be recognized as a very special employee who sets a new goal for all other salespeople to meet.

Format	Group Competition
Game Play	Olympic Trials are held in five separate sales categories. To spur on competition among the sales staff, the three top performers in each category at the end of the Trials are given awards. The top performer in each category receives a Gold Medal award. Thereafter, any individual who sets a new Sales World Record in any category receives a new Gold Medal award. Sales World Record holders are recognized on a Go for the Gold! record board.

Basic Rules

- Olympic Trials are held in five separate categories:
  - Largest Weekly Average Sale
  - Largest Weekly Items per Sale
  - Largest Weekly Sales per Hour
  - Largest Weekly Total Sales Volume
  - Largest Single Sale to One Customer

- Management determines the time period for the Trials (one month is a good trial period). To increase the competition during the Trials, the top statistic in each category is continually posted.

- At the end of the Trials, Gold, Silver, and Bronze Medal prizes are awarded to the top three performers in each category. The Gold Medal winners' names and winning statistics are posted on a Go for the Gold! record board.

- After the Trials, for the duration of the Olympics, any salesperson who beats one of the top statistics posted replaces the corresponding Gold Medal winner on the record board and receives a Gold Medal prize.

- The Olympics may be held within one store or among the stores in a chain or region for an indefinite period of time, or for a set period of time on an annual or quarterly basis. For the greatest effect, we recommend a huge promotion of the Trials, and running the game indefinitely, but that will depend on your store and your staff. For the competition, choose the statistics that are most appropriate for your business.

Suggested Timeframe

One month, up to an ongoing contest

Rewards

Depending on the number of competitors and the difficulty of the goals set, use medium to big rewards (see appendix). You also might look into obtaining Gold, Silver, and Bronze Medals from a local trophy shop.

Promoting the Game

- Before you begin the game, make certain you have established a way to track each statistic you will measure. Individual Daily Performance Summaries, averaged out at the end of the week and reviewed by management, are suggested.

- Begin the Trials with a big promotion, including an official notice that the games are about to begin, an "Olympic Torch," and the theme music from the games. Opening ceremonies could center on a review of sales training or techniques to help people improve their statistics. If this is a multiple-store contest, a visit from the district or regional manager may be appropriate.

- During the Trials, post the best statistics each day. This will make for more competition.

- At the end of the Trials, reward the medalists in a ceremony. Include a three-elevation stand, just like in the real Olympics. Play the National Anthem.

- Make your Go for the Gold! record board stand out. Post it in a very noticeable place, possibly behind your cash desk, where customers can see it. Include the names of the current Gold Medalists, the dates the records were set, and the winning statistics. Each time a new World Record is set, replace the former record holder with the new one. If the contest is being held between more than one store, each store should update its record board as required, noting the home store of the medalist(s).

Props and Supplies

- Statistics tally board(s) for the Trials

- Go for the Gold! record board(s)

- Prizes and medals

- Olympic props (three-elevation stand, torch, music, etc.)

Variations

Throughout the contest, recognize the new Silver and Bronze Medalists. This is more difficult to track, but for single-store games it may be a good option to get more people involved.

SCAVENGER HUNT

Scavenger Hunt is a good review for new employees after they receive store orientation. Larger stores, or stores with an extensive array of smaller or frequently changing merchandise, can use it to quiz salespeople about the location of key items. Used either way, Scavenger Hunt is a fun and exciting game. It illustrates the importance of walking the floor and knowing the location of each and every item in the store.

Format	Individual or Group Competition
Game Play	Salespeople must find each item on a list provided by management. The first person (or team) to find all the items wins.

Basic Rules

- Create a list of "lost" items for each player or team. Include an equal number of items on each list, but avoid placing the same item on more than one list, so that the players will not chase each other around to find the location of any one item. For new employees, you might include items such as extra charge-sales drafts, light bulbs, and bags and boxes. Or you can focus the game on new merchandise that salespeople need to locate.

- Give one list to each player (or team). Have each player begin at the same time, in the same place. Your "starting line" could be the front door or your office.

- The first player or team to find all the items on their list wins. Or you may choose to set a time limit and award the prize to the player or team that finds the most items.

Suggested Timeframe   Depending on the number of players and your store's traffic pattern, you might choose to play this game either when the store is open or when it is closed.

Rewards   Small reward to the winner (see appendix)

Promoting the Game   When you explain the game, talk about how important it is for salespeople to be prepared each day, prior to their shifts. Salespeople need to arrive early and walk the floor to note any changes in merchandise locations, displays, pricing, and so forth.

Props and Supplies
- Scavenger Hunt lists
- Prizes

OPENING THE SALE GAME

Since customers sometimes react negatively to salespeople who approach them, your sales staff need to have a wealth of effective opening lines at their disposal. This game requires your salespeople to develop as many opening lines as they can while conforming to the three rules for effective opening lines. If you and your staff are not familiar with the Opening the Sale section of The Friedman Group's Gold Star Selling Course, you will want to work through it prior to running this game.

Format   Individual or Group Competition

Game Play   The entire sales staff stands in a line, with the manager standing in the center. The first person closest to each side of the manager must "open the sale"—each of the two salespeople must deliver an effective opening line. After doing this, they go to the end of their respective lines and the next two salespeople open the sale in the same fashion. Each opening line must follow the three rules for opening lines, and none can stem from the same general topic. Salespeople who deliver lines that don't conform to the rules must sit down. The last person left standing wins.

Basic Rules
- Line up your sales staff, stand in the center of the line, and have the two resulting lines face each other. Remain in the center to referee the game.

- The salesperson at the front of each line must deliver one opening line that follows the three rules for opening lines:

    1. Opening lines must have nothing to do with business.

    2. Opening lines should be questions, to encourage conversation.

3. Opening lines should be unique, sincere, or different enough to cause a conversation.

- No opening line may stem from the same topic as a previous opening line (e.g., no two lines focusing on another person's clothing, etc.).

- Salespeople who deliver effective opening lines go to the end of their respective lines and wait their turn to play again. Salespeople who repeat a topic or who do not follow one of the rules must sit down.

- The last person standing is the winner.

Suggested Timeframe

Hold the game during a store meeting, when the store is closed. The time you'll need to play the game depends on the size of your sales staff.

Rewards

Give a small reward to the winner (see appendix).

Promoting the Game

- Play this game as a follow-up to training on how to open the sale.

- Announce the game one week in advance to allow people to practice opening lines. Walk the floor the week before the game, and coach people who need help with their opening skills.

Props and Supplies

- Whiteboard or flip chart to list opening lines so that you can check for duplicates

- Prize for the winner

THE PROBING GAME

The best way to satisfy a customer's wants, needs, and desires is to ask questions—to probe for answers. Probing questions are open-ended questions; they require more than a yes-or-no answer. Use this game as a follow-up exercise to the Probing section of The Friedman Group's Gold Star Selling Course to further develop your sales staff's probing skills.

Format

Individual Competition

Game Play

The entire sales staff stands in a line. A salesperson is chosen at random to begin the game. The manager holds up an item and says, "I've been looking for one of these . . . ." The first salesperson must ask a probing question to learn more about the "customer's" wants, needs, and desires. The game continues on down the line until a salesperson cannot think of a new probing question. That salesperson sits down, and the game begins again with a new item. The last salesperson standing is the winner.

Basic Rules

- Salespeople line up in random order. The manager chooses a number out of a container to begin the game.

- The manager holds up an item. Playing the role of customer, the manager says, "I've been looking for one of these . . . ." The salesperson who corresponds to the chosen number begins the game by asking a probing question about the "customer's" wants, needs, and desires.

- The next person in line must ask another probing question. The game continues in this fashion until someone cannot think of a new probing question.

- The first person who cannot come up with a new question sits down. The game begins again. The manager pulls another number out of the container and holds up another item.

- The last person left standing is the winner.

- All probing questions must be open-ended (i.e., will not result in a yes-or-no answer) and designed to find facts about the customer's wants, needs, and desires (see sample probing questions).

Suggested Timeframe

Hold the game during a store meeting, when the store is closed to customers. The time you'll need depends on the size of your staff.

Rewards

Small reward to the winner (see appendix)

Promoting the Game

- Announce the game one store meeting in advance, allowing the salespeople time to practice their probing skills. Talk about the importance of probing questions and how they can benefit the store, salespeople, and customers. Review what constitutes a good probing question.

- Walk the floor the week before the game, and coach salespeople who need help with their probing skills.

Props and Supplies

- Slips of paper and a container for choosing the order of play

- Merchandise for the "customer"

- Dry-erase board or flip chart to track probing questions, to avoid duplicates

- Prize for the winner

PROBING QUESTIONS

WHO:

Who are you shopping for?

Who told you about our store?

Who is your favorite manufacturer/designer?

WHAT:

What brings you into our store today?

What's the special occasion?

What kind do you have now?

What would you like this one to do differently?

What have you seen before that you've really liked?

What colors/styles do you prefer?

What do you think your friend/husband/wife would like best?

WHEN:

When is the special occasion?

When did you begin shopping?

When do you need it by?

WHERE:

Where have you seen one before?

Where will it be used/worn?

Where is the special event taking place?

HOW:

How did you hear about us/our store?

How often do you shop/update your wardrobe?

How did you decide on this model/brand?

How many people will use it?

WHY:

Why do you want a red/blue/yellow one?

Why do you want cotton/wool, rather than silk/rayon?

Why do you like that specific brand/model/style?

Why are you concerned about durability?

TELL ME:

Tell me about your husband/wife/child.

Tell me about your plans for redecorating/vacationing/holding the party.

Tell me more about the problems you've had in the past.

PROBING QUESTIONS

SKILL

This variation on The Probing Game gives your salespeople further practice in developing a wide range of probing questions.

Format

Individual or Group Competition

Game Play

The sales staff is divided up into two or more teams. Each team is given five minutes to write out probing questions on a flip chart. The winning team is the one with the most questions at the end of five minutes.

Basic Rules

- Divide your sales staff up into two or more teams.

- Give each team one flip chart page or piece of newsprint and markers for each team member.

- Each team divides their page into six sections: *Who, What, When, Where, Why,* and *How.*

- Teams have five minutes to record probing questions under each category. The questions must be open-ended and designed to find facts about customers' wants, needs, and desires (see sample probing questions from The Probing Game).

- The team with the most questions at the end of five minutes wins.

- Teams should take care when discussing questions so that other teams will not overhear them.

Suggested Timeframe

Hold the game during a store meeting when the store is closed to customers.

Rewards　　　　　　　　　Small rewards to the winning team members (see appendix)

Promoting the Game

- Play this game as a follow-up to The Probing Game or any time you feel your people need practice with probing questions. Be sure you review the rules for probing questions prior to beginning the game.

- Walk the floor before the game, and coach salespeople who need help with their probing skills.

- Use a stopwatch to time the game and a whistle to announce when it's time to stop.

Props and Supplies

- Flip chart pages or newsprint

- Markers

- Stopwatch/whistle

- Prizes for the winners

Variations　　　　　　　Create an individual format by providing individual sheets of paper.

GUESS THE ITEM

SKILL

Guess the Item is another exercise to develop probing skills. Salespeople use probing questions to guess the identity of store merchandise. The better salespeople are at asking probing questions, the fewer they will need to ask in order to guess the correct identity of each item.

Format

Individual Competition

Game Play

Each salesperson tries to guess the identity of an item in the store using as few probing questions as possible. The salesperson who uses the fewest probing questions to guess the item wins.

Basic Rules

- Write down an item in your store on a piece of paper.

- One at a time, in private, have each salesperson use probing questions to guess the identity of the item.

- Each probing question must be open-ended (i.e., will not result in a yes-or-no answer) and designed to find facts about customer wants, needs, and desires (see sample probing questions from The Probing Game).

- Invalid questions are not answered, but are added to the count of questions asked by each salesperson.

- Keep a record of the number of questions it takes each salesperson to guess the item. Award a small prize to the salesperson who uses the fewest questions and correctly identifies the item. Salespeople must identify the exact style, size, and so forth.

Suggested Timeframe	Hold the game during a store meeting, when the store is closed to customers, or when the store is slow and you can rotate individual salespeople on and off the selling floor to play the game.
Rewards	Give a small reward to the winner (see appendix). This could be the secret item itself.
Promoting the Game	• Play this game as a follow-up to The Probing Game or any time you feel your people need practice with probing questions. Be sure you review the rules for probing questions prior to beginning the game.
	• Walk the floor before the game, and coach salespeople who need help with their probing skills.
	• Each time a salesperson finishes asking questions, announce the total number of questions asked, and encourage the next salesperson to do even better.
Props and Supplies	• Secret item
	• Prize for the winner
Variations	Play the game once each day for an entire week using a different item each day. Award a larger prize to the salesperson who guesses the most items using the fewest total questions.

PRICES BY MEMORY

SKILL

Salespeople gain instant credibility when they can quote prices and price differentials without looking at item tags or referring to a price list. This game will cultivate your sales staff's ability to quote correct prices.

Format	Individual Competition
Game Play	The sales staff stands in a line and the manager asks each person the price of a particular item. Salespeople who answer correctly remain in the game while those who answer with the wrong price must sit down. The salesperson who remains standing at the end of the game is the winner.
Basic Rules	• Select a wide variety of merchandise from your store. The quantity you select will have an effect on how long this game will take to play. Make certain you know the price of each selected item.
	• Have your sales staff stand in a line. Moving from person to person in the line, hold up (or mention) an item and ask for its price. Salespeople who answer correctly stay in the game. Salespeople who give you the wrong price must sit down.
	• The person left standing at the end of the game wins.
Suggested Timeframe	Hold the game during a store meeting when the store is closed. The time you'll need to play the game depends on the size of your sales staff and the number of items you choose.
Rewards	Give a small reward to the winner (see appendix). You might award one of the items from the game.

Promoting the Game

Announce the game one week in advance to allow people to study the merchandise on the floor. Emphasize the benefits of quoting prices without referring to a list or item tags. Walk the floor the week before the game, and quiz people on pricing.

Props and Supplies

- Items for price quiz
- Prize for the winner

THE PRODUCT-FEATURE GAME

In this product knowledge game, salespeople are asked to identify the correct product features for the items they sell. This is a good exercise for determining which staff members need additional training in product knowledge. This game will also give your staff increased incentive to learn all they can about your store's merchandise.

Format

Individual Competition

Game Play

The entire sales staff stands in a line facing the store manager. The manager holds up a variety of merchandise, listing features that *could be* associated with each item. Each staff member responds "True" or "False" to whether each item has the feature mentioned. Salespeople who answer incorrectly must sit down. The last person standing is the winner.

Basic Rules

- Select a wide variety of merchandise from your store. Include both older and newer items, slow and fast sellers. Create a list of possible product features for each one. Include features that each product actually has, and features that each product could have, but does not (e.g., a stereo system with Dolby noise reduction, a television that's cable-ready, etc.).

- Line up your sales staff facing you. Hold up the items, and recite the list of features for each one. After you say each feature, staff members must respond "True" by raising a hand, or "False" by doing nothing. Count to three, and require the responses at the count of four. Everyone must respond at the same time.

- Salespeople who respond incorrectly must sit down. Continue with the game. The last person standing wins.

Suggested Timeframe

Hold the game during a store meeting when the store is closed. The time you'll need to play the game depends on the size of your sales staff and the number of items you choose.

Rewards

Give a small reward to the winner (see appendix). You might award one of the items from the game.

Promoting the Game

- Play this game as a follow-up to product knowledge training, and regularly as part of your store meetings. This will help your staff stay educated about products and current/new features promoted by your industry.

- Announce the game one week in advance to allow people to study the merchandise on the floor. Walk the floor the week before the game, and quiz people on product knowledge.

Props and Supplies

- Items and list of true and false features

- Prizes for the winner

NAME THAT PRODUCT

SKILL

This is another product knowledge game in which you list off the features for a number of items. Each salesperson tries to be the first to guess the item you are describing. The more a salesperson knows about your store's merchandise, the greater his or her chances of winning.

Format	Individual Competition
Game Play	The manager creates a list of features of a number of items in the store. During the game, the features of each item are recited one by one. The first salesperson to call out the correct name, style, model number, and so on is awarded one point. The salesperson with the most points at the end of the game wins.

Basic Rules

- Select a wide variety of merchandise from your store. The quantity you select will have an effect on how long this game will take to play. Create a list of features for each item. Begin with more general descriptive features and move toward more specific features at the end.

- Gather your sales staff together. Recite the list of features for each item, pausing briefly after each feature. The first person to guess the exact item (including style or model number, if necessary) is awarded one point. Record point totals on a tally board.

- The person with the most points at the end of the game wins.

Suggested Timeframe

Hold the game during a store meeting when the store is closed. The time you'll need to play the game depends on the size of your sales staff and the number of items you choose.

Rewards

Give a small reward to the winner (see appendix). You might award one of the items from the game.

Promoting the Game

- Play this game as a follow-up to product knowledge training, and regularly as part of your store meetings. This will help your staff stay educated about products and current/ new features promoted by your industry.

- Announce the game one week in advance to allow people to study the merchandise on the floor. Walk the floor the week before the game, and quiz people on product knowledge.

Props and Supplies

- List of features for each item

- Whiteboard or flip chart to record point totals

- Prize for the winner

THE FABG GAME

SKILL

FABG stands for Feature-Advantage-Benefit-Grabber. The FABG is a key element in The Friedman Group's Gold Star Selling Course, and if you don't know about FABGs, you should. FABGs are used in the product demonstration to add value to the merchandise being shown. Even though we've provided a brief explanation at the end of this game, in order to run this game you must be an FABG expert. If you're thoroughly familiar with FABGs, and you've taught your staff how to use them and want to make certain they are using them properly, this is a great game to play.

Format

Individual Competition

Game Play

A variety of merchandise is placed on a table. The entire sales staff stands in a line. The first salesperson chooses an item and must recite an FABG for that item, beginning with "One of the nice things about this . . ." and ending with a grabber. Each salesperson in line repeats these actions. No FABG may be duplicated. Any salesperson who recites an incorrect or duplicate FABG must sit down. The last person standing is the winner.

Basic Rules

- Choose a variety of items and display them on a table.

- Have your sales staff form a line behind the table. The first person must choose an item and recite an FABG for that item.

- Each successive person must choose an item and recite an FABG for it. No FABGs may be duplicated. Salespeople who duplicate or recite an incorrect FABG (e.g., switching advantages and benefits) must sit down. Salespeople who remain standing go to the end of the line and wait their turn.

- The last person left standing is the winner.

Suggested Timeframe	Hold the game during a store meeting when the store is closed. The length of the game will depend on your staff size.
Rewards	Give a small reward to the winner (see appendix). This could be one of the items on the table.
Props and Supplies	• Merchandise for the table • Prize for the winner
Variations	Play this game as a follow-up to training on FABGs. This will prepare your staff to use FABGs with customers on the selling floor.

FEATURE–ADVANTAGE–BENEFIT–GRABBER (FABG)

Feature: A noticeable part or characteristic of an item (e.g., what it's made from, where it was made, its color or style, etc.). Each item we sell is composed of various features the manufacturer selected to be similar to or different from the competition.

Advantage: The advantage is directly tied to the feature. In general, the advantage is what the customer gains by having a feature versus not having that feature.

Benefit: The benefit is tied to the advantage. A benefit is, by definition, "What will the advantage do for the customer?"

Grabber: In the grabber, the benefit is restated to the customer as a question to elicit a positive response.

(continued)

(continued)

For example:

Item:	Hula Hoop
Feature:	Perfectly round
Advantage:	Easy to spin
Benefit:	You'll have fun
Grabber:	You like to have fun, don't you?

FABGs begin with "One of the nice things about this . . . ." This implies that there are many nice things about the item.

Put together, the above FABG could sound like this:

"One of the nice things about this hula hoop is that the manufacturer designed it to be perfectly round, so that it's very easy to spin. The easier it is to spin, the more fun you'll have—you like to have fun, don't you?"

To check FABGs, you can use the "Which means it down and why it up" test. For example:

The hula hoop is perfectly round (which means) it's easy to spin (which means) you'll have fun. (Why?) Because the hula hoop is easy to spin. (Why?) Because it's perfectly round.

If you insert "which means" between the FAB parts on the way down and insert "why" on the way up and it makes sense, then your FAB is probably correct.

FABG SCRAMBLE

FABG Scramble gives salespeople further practice in the proper construction of FABGs. Salespeople commonly confuse advantages and benefits, and may make other mistakes in constructing their FABGs. This Scramble game is a good way to make sure none of your salespeople are doing this. In order to play this game, you'll first have to train your salespeople on the use of FABGs, as explained in the Demonstration section of The Friedman Group's Gold Star Selling Course.

Format	Individual Competition
Game Play	Salespeople are given five FABGs for one item, scrambled in no particular order. The first person to properly unscramble all the FABGs wins a prize.

Basic Rules

- Choose an item from your selling floor and write five FABGs for it.

- Scramble the FABGs on a piece of paper and indicate the item described by the FABGs. Below the FABGs, include spaces for salespeople to unscramble the FABGs in their proper order (see example).

- Make a photocopy of the quiz for each salesperson. Do not let salespeople see the quiz prior to the game.

- Have all the salespeople sit down at the same time. Hand out the quizzes, face down, and have the salespeople turn over their quizzes when you start the game.

- Have salespeople turn in their quizzes as soon as they are done. The first person to correctly complete the quiz wins a prize.

Suggested Timeframe Hold the game during a store meeting when the store is closed.

Rewards Give a small reward to the winner (see appendix). This could be the item you wrote the FABGs for.

Promoting the Game Play this game as a follow-up to training on FABGs. This will prepare your staff to use FABGs with customers on the selling floor.

Props and Supplies
- Master list of FABGs and quizzes for salespeople
- Prize for the winner

SCRAMBLE, WITH ANSWERS	
Instructions: Rearrange the scrambled FABGs below in the correct order to create five FABGs. (The item described is a house.)	
Numerous windows	One could be used as a den
Swim whenever you feel like it	No need to change carpet when decorating
Will blend with many different colors	Swimming pool in the back yard
Nice having your own private getaway, isn't it?	That beats having to go to the gym, right?
Allow sunlight in	Stockade-fenced yard
That would be convenient, wouldn't it?	Giving you the ultimate in privacy
Four bedrooms	That can save you money in the long run, don't you think?
And natural light is nice, isn't it?	Neighbors can't see in
Creating a bright atmosphere	Convenient for exercising
Neutral-color carpeting	Quiet place to work on weekends

F: _____

A: _____

B: _____

G: _____

F: _____

A: _____

B: _____

G: _____

F: _____

A: _____

B: _____

G: _____

F: _____

A: _____

B: _____

G: _____

F: _____

A: _____

B: _____

G: _____

ANSWERS

F: Numerous windows

A: Allow sunlight in

B: Creating a bright atmosphere

G: And natural light is nice, isn't it?

F: Swimming pool in the back yard

A: Swim whenever you feel like it

B: Convenient for exercising

G: That beats having to go to the gym, right?

F: Four bedrooms

A: One could be used as a den

B: Quiet place to work on weekends

G: That would be convenient, wouldn't it?

F: Stockade-fenced yard

A: Neighbors can't see in

B: Giving you the ultimate in privacy

G: Nice having your own private getaway, isn't it?

F: Neutral-color carpeting

A: Will blend with many different colors

B: No need to change carpet when redecorating

G: That can save you money in the long run, don't you think?

THE ADD-ON GAME

SKILL

Add-on sales make your store more profitable. If your salespeople are paid on a commission basis, add-on sales also mean that your salespeople make more money. This game will help to stretch your sales staff's capacity for adding on. In the Add-on Game, salespeople are asked to come up with all possible add-on items for a list of primary items.

Format

Individual Competition

Game Play

The entire sales staff stands in a line. A salesperson is chosen at random to begin the game. The manager names a primary item and the first salesperson must name an add-on for that item. The next salesperson in line must name another add-on for that same item. The game continues down the line in this fashion until someone cannot name an add-on. That person sits down and the manager begins again with a new primary item. The last salesperson standing is the winner.

Basic Rules

- Salespeople line up in random order. The manager picks a number out of a container to begin the game.

- The manager names a primary item. The salesperson who corresponds to the chosen number begins the game by naming an add-on to the primary item.

- The next person in line must name another add-on to the primary item. The game continues in this fashion until someone cannot name an add-on.

- The first person who cannot name an add-on sits down. The game begins again. The manager pulls another number out of the container and names a new primary item.

- The last person left standing is the winner.

Suggested Timeframe   Hold the game during a store meeting, when the store is closed to customers. The time you'll need depends on the size of your staff.

Rewards   Small reward to the winner (see appendix)

Promoting the Game
- Announce the game one store meeting in advance, allowing salespeople time to practice their add-on skills. Talk about the importance of adding on and how it can benefit the store, salespeople, and customers. Review add-on techniques.

- Walk the floor the week before the game and coach salespeople who need help with their add-on skills.

- Follow up the game with another game or contest to reward salespeople for their items-per-sale performance (e.g., Items-per-Sale Pennant or Items-per-Sale Contest).

Props and Supplies
- Slips of paper and a container for choosing the order of play

- List of primary merchandise items

- Dry-erase board or flip chart to track named add-on items, to avoid duplicates

- Prize for the winner

ADDING-ON-TO-CLOSE

The Assumptive Add-on Close, explained in The Friedman Group's Gold Star Selling Course, is a very effective technique for closing the sale. The salesperson simply suggests appropriate add-ons, thereby "assuming" the customer has already decided to buy the primary item under consideration. This technique helps salespeople close their sales in a friendly, nonthreatening manner, and also gives them a chance to increase their add-on sales. In this game, salespeople see how many Assumptive Add-on Closes they can think of in a set period of time. We've provided some examples at the end of this game. Still, you'll want to take your salespeople through the Gold Star Selling Course before playing the game.

Format   Individual Competition

Game Play   The manager chooses a selection of primary item sales in the store. Salespeople choose one item and must recite as many Assumptive Add-on Closes as possible for that item within a set time limit. The salesperson who names the most Assumptive Add-on Closes wins.

Basic Rules
- Choose a selection of primary item sales for the game so that you will have at least one per salesperson.

- Select salespeople in random order to play the game (draw names out of a container, etc.). Set an equal time limit for each player (e.g., two minutes).

- Each player selects one item and recites as many Assumptive Add-on Closes as he or she can think of. The manager keeps a record of the number on a tally board.

- After everyone has had a chance to play, the salesperson with the most Assumptive Add-on Closes wins a prize.

Suggested Timeframe	Hold the game during a store meeting, when the store is closed to customers. The time you'll need depends on the size of your staff.
Rewards	Small reward to the winner (see appendix)

Promoting the Game

- Announce the game one store meeting in advance, allowing salespeople time to practice their Assumptive Add-on Close skills. Talk about the importance of adding on to close the sale and how this can benefit the store, salespeople, and customers.

- Walk the floor the week before the game and coach salespeople who need help.

Props and Supplies

- Slips of paper and a container for choosing the order of play

- Primary sale items

- Dry-erase board or flip chart to tally the number of Assumptive Add-on Closes for each player

- Prize for the winner

ASSUMPTIVE ADD-ON CLOSE EXAMPLES

The Assumptive Add-on Close has five parts:

1. **How about**

   Salespeople start their trial closes with "How about . . ." to form a friendly question.

2. **The Enhancer**

   The enhancer makes the add-on item more desirable to the customer.

(continued)

(continued)

3. The Add-On

This is the add-on item itself. Salespeople should use clues discovered about the customer during probing to suggest an appropriate add-on item.

4. Must Have

This is a word or phrase that makes the add-on item appear to be an essential thing for the customer to have.

5. Possession

Salespeople add the word "you" or "your" to describe the primary item at the end of the trial close to give customers automatic possession of it.

Here's an example of an Assumptive Add-on Close. Each part is numbered.

1	2	3	4	5

{How about} this {perfectly matched} {scarf} {to complete the look} of {your} new outfit?

More examples:

- How about a convenient carrying case to safeguard your new MP3 player from unexpected bumps?

- How about this specially formulated leather-treatment kit to protect your new briefcase?

- How about this fashionable tennis bracelet to enhance the look of your new watch?

- How about a coordinating dust ruffle to accent your comforter and create the look you wanted to achieve?

THE PERSONAL TRADE GAME

SKILL

When a customer visits your store and asks to see a specific salesperson, you can bet that salesperson has a habit of delivering outstanding customer service and following up that service with calls, letters, and other personal-trade tools. Personal trade can greatly increase your store's sales, and it also makes selling more rewarding. This game directly rewards salespeople for working to develop their own personal trade.

Format Individual Competition

Game Play Each time salespeople send a follow-up letter or thank-you note to a customer, they are given a special coupon. Coupons are coded to correspond with each salesperson's name. A customer who returns to the store with a coupon may redeem it for a percentage or dollar amount off the price of his or her next purchase. At the end of the game period, the coupons are tallied and the salesperson with the most redeemed coupons wins.

Basic Rules
- Create some sort of small certificate for a percentage or dollar amount off a customer's next purchase. Code the coupons with your sales staff's initials. Go to a print shop for a more professional look, or use desktop publishing software, a personal computer, good paper, and a photocopy machine.

- Each time a salesperson sends a thank-you note or some type of follow-up letter to a customer, give the salesperson a coupon to enclose.

- At the end of the game, count the number of coupons redeemed for each salesperson. Award a prize to the salesperson who has sold to the most repeat customers.

Suggested Timeframe	Tally the coupons at the end of one month. Or you may choose to have an ongoing game and award a prize to the salesperson with the most coupons each month.
Rewards	Medium rewards (see appendix)
Promoting the Game	• Use the game as a follow-up to training in personal-trade techniques. Give salespeople a month or so to practice after the training is complete before you run the game, and coach staff members who are having trouble.
	• Support your staff by providing notepaper and envelopes that match the coupons you create.
Props and Supplies	• Coupons
	• Matching notepaper and envelopes

QUESTION-AND-ANSWER GAME

SKILL

If you want to run a skill-development game that covers a wide range of topics, try this one. Players who meet sales goals draw cards. Each card has a different product knowledge, operations, or salesmanship question written on it. Salespeople who answer questions correctly are awarded points, and points are redeemed for cash or prizes.

Format Individual Competition

Game Play Players who meet sales goals choose skill-development questions written on cards (see examples from Retail Jeopardy). The questions are worth points based on their difficulty. Players who answer questions correctly earn points, which are redeemed for cash or prizes at the end of the game.

Basic Rules

- Create a list of skill-development questions in three areas: product knowledge, salesmanship, and operations. Assign each question a point value based on its difficulty (one = easy; two = medium; three = difficult).

- Write each question and its point value on an index card. Sort the cards by level of difficulty and place them in piles.

- Determine which sales goals will be used for the game. Players might earn the right to draw a card when they meet their daily average sale goal, or they might draw a card when they sell an item from a specific category.

- Players choose from one of the three piles. Those who answer a question correctly receive the corresponding number of points.

- Keep a running tally of each player's earnings. At the end of the game, award cash or prizes based on points earned.

Suggested Timeframe	One week
Rewards	Small, medium, and big prizes, based on points earned (see appendix), or cash

Promoting the Game

- Post a tally board to track each player's point earnings.

- Post a list of point values and the prizes to be won.

- Use the game as a follow-up to training and focus the questions on the training materials.

Props and Supplies

- Tally board to post point earnings

- Point-prize chart

- Index cards

- List of questions

Variations

Instead of using index cards, write out the questions in list form. Players trade their points for time (e.g., 40 points = two minutes). At the end of the game, each player uses his or her time to answer as many questions as possible. The player who answers the most questions in the time allotted wins a prize.

The game board shows the following categories and point values:

THE PRECHECK	OPENING THE SALE	PROBING	DEMONSTRATION	TRIAL CLOSE	OBJECTIONS
100	100	100	100	100	100
200	200	200	200	200	200
300	300	300		300	300
400	400	400		400	400
500	500	500		500	500

RETAIL JEOPARDY

SKILL

Retail Jeopardy is an excellent skill-development game. It takes some time and effort to set up, but the return you'll get is worth the effort. You can adapt the game to focus on product knowledge, store operations, or salesmanship, depending on the question–answer pairs you use.

Format

Group Competition

Game Play

Team members play for points by providing the correct questions for the answers revealed on a Jeopardy game board. Each correct question–answer pair is worth a specific number of points. The team with the most points at the end of the game wins.

Basic Rules

- Questions and answers are listed under separate categories. Each correct question–answer pair is worth a specific number of points (see example).

- Three teams play for points by providing the correct questions for the answers.

- The manager reveals one answer at a time, calling on one player from each team to play each round. The first player to "ring in" gets to guess the question for the answer revealed. If the question is correct, the player's team is awarded the corresponding number of points. If the question is incorrect, the player's team loses that number of points, and the other players in the round are given an opportunity to ring in. Once players ring in, they have 10 seconds to respond.

- As soon as a correct question is identified (or if no player chooses to ring in within 10 seconds), the manager chooses another player from each team to play another round, revealing another answer. Answers are revealed in order from lowest to highest point value within each category.

- When all the answers have been revealed, the team with the most points wins.

- Players must phrase their response in the form of a question (e.g., "What is . . . ?" or "What are . . . ?"). If they do not do this, their response is considered incorrect, points are deducted, and the other players have a chance to ring in.

- Teammates may not coach each other and must remain silent while each round is in play.

Suggested Timeframe

Hold the game during a store meeting, when the store is closed to customers. The time you'll need depends on the size of your staff and the number of question–answer pairs you create.

Rewards

Small to medium rewards for the winning team members (see appendix), or a team award (e.g., lunch at a local restaurant, a pizza, etc.).

Promoting the Game

- Hang a large Jeopardy board in your stockroom, break-room, or office.

  - Write each answer category along the top edge of a large, heavy poster board. Cut one square in the poster board for each answer, grouping the squares under the appropriate answer category.

  - Place a second poster board, in a different color, underneath the first. Using a heavy marker, write the answers in their correct locations. Glue the two poster boards together.

  - Attach Velcro to both the Jeopardy board and the cut-out squares so that you can use the squares to hide each answer.

  - Write the point value of each answer on the front of the square that hides it.

  - Write each question–answer pair on an index card to help you judge the contest.

- Create a method for players to ring in when they think they have the correct question. You could use bells (make sure each bell makes a different sound), or fill glasses with water so that each glass makes a different sound when tapped with a pencil.

- Allow teams to choose names. Write the name of each team, the team members, and the order of play on a tally board. Keep track of points earned (or lost) by each team member, and a running tally of each team's total points.

Props and Supplies

- List of question–answer pairs in five categories

- Jeopardy board

- Ringers

- Stopwatch to time players

- Prizes for the winning team

- Tally board to keep track of each team's score

Variations

- Write "Double Jeopardy" on two pieces of construction paper and cover two of your answers with it. Before you reveal a bonus square, allow players to wager their team's points on whether they can come up with the correct question. The individual player is responsible for the wager. This is not a team decision.

- Hold a "Final Jeopardy" round in which each team, as a group, wagers points on whether they can come up with the correct question for one final answer. Make this a difficult question–answer pair. Allow each team five minutes to come up with their question and the number of points they will wager.

- Make two or more squares "Video Jeopardy" squares. Show a brief lecture section from the Gold Star Selling Course and have the player guess which section the lecture is from. The response must be in the form of a question to be correct (e.g., "What is the Daily Precheck?").

- Create a combination skill-development/sales-performance game. Each person plays individually, earning the right to play upon meeting a specific sales goal. Hold the game while the store is open and announce play each time someone meets a goal. Allow salespeople to choose which square to reveal, or make each sales goal correspond to a different square.

QUESTION–ANSWER PAIRS	
Product Knowledge	
100	Stronger and more durable than a soft-wood frame. *What is a hardwood frame?*
200	The best cushioning material available. *What is high-resiliency, solid, 100% virgin polyurethane foam?*
300	Soft, but not hypoallergenic. *What is down padding and cushioning?*
400	Stronger than wood itself. *What is the glue used for furniture joints?*
500	The best way to sell a room. *What is show a vignette, rather than just one piece?*
Store Operations	
100	Don't use these as trash containers. *What are transfer cartons?*
200	Ten minutes go by, and there's no one there to open the store. *What is time to call the district manager?*

(continued)

Store Operations (*continued*)

300	When you don't have the right size for a customer.
	What is call the nearest store for a special order?
400	When it turns blue on the edge.
	What is how you know that it's time to change the register tape?
500	Every Wednesday.
	What is when we receive our ad flyers each week?

Sales and Customer Service

100	Smile and say hello.
	What is how we greet every customer who enters our store?
200	"How may I help you?"
	What is the wrong question to ask customers?
300	A handwritten thank-you note.
	What is one of the best ways to set yourself and your store apart from others with your customers?
400	"How about a (this) to go with your (that)?"
	What is the Assumptive Add-on Close?
500	Getting past customer resistance.
	What is one (or the primary) goal of opening the sale?

Loss Prevention	
100	Approach and greet each customer.
	What is one of the best ways to prevent shoplifting?
200	Count and inspect each article.
	What should be done before a customer enters a fitting room?
300	Items that are $100 and above.
	What is the value of merchandise that must be chained or locked in a case?
400	Alert a manager and do not take your eyes off the person.
	What are steps you take when you spot a potential shoplifter?
500	Stop all transactions and call a manager.
	What should cashiers do when a customer claims to have received incorrect change?

I sincerely hope that you will use and enjoy the games from this collection, both to make your store more profitable and to help your sales staff make the most out of their work each day. Games and contests add fun, excitement, and life to retail sales—qualities that you, your staff, and your customers are sure to benefit from.

Here are some ideas for rewards. Read through the lists for small, medium, and big rewards. Think about what your staff values most, and add to these lists. Be creative. For more ideas, review Chapter Four of this book, "Making Your Case and Establishing a Reward System."

As always, good luck and good selling!

Small Rewards

- Lottery Tickets
- Movie Tickets
- Cash Awards (Up to $25)
- Jar of Candy or Nuts
- Extra Employee Discount
- Gift Certificates to a Fast-Food Restaurant
- Free Lunch at a Local Restaurant

- No Housekeeping Duties for One Week

- Six-Pack of Soft Drinks

- Logo Merchandise from Local School/Team: T-Shirt, Sweatshirt, Cap, Tote Bag

- Music (CD or File Download)

- Certificates for Free Desserts/Snacks: Mrs. Field's, Baskin-Robbins, Wetzel's, Godiva

- Desk Accessories: Pen/Pencil Cup, Letter Opener, Picture Frame, Lamp, Coffee Mug

- Bottle of Wine

- Trivia Calendar

- Umbrella

- Business-Card Holder: Desk or Wallet

- Hardcover Book or Bestseller: *No Thanks, I'm Just Looking!*, Popular Authors, Industry-Related Topics, Blank Book, Set of Paperbacks, Audio Books, Reference (Dictionary/Thesaurus)

- Subscription to Industry-Related Magazine

- Popular Movie on DVD

- Refrigerator Magnets

- Battery-Operated Personal Fan

- Holiday-Themed Merchandise: Tie, Pin, Scarf, Hosiery/Socks, Hat

- Set of Gift Teas or Coffee

- Free Round of Golf/Miniature Golf
- Puzzles
- "Write Your Own Schedule" for a Week
- Bumper Sticker
- Reserved Parking Space for a Month

Medium Rewards

- Gift Certificate
- Dinner at a Favorite Restaurant
- Sporting Goods or Game Equipment: Tennis Racquet, Inline Skates
- Handheld Electronic Game
- Cash Award (Up to $100)
- Binoculars
- Small or Portable Electronic Equipment: Clock Radio, iPod Speakers, Cell Phone Charger, MP3 Player, DVD Player, Digital Recorder

Big Rewards

- Double Commission for a Week (or Reasonably Specified Time Period)
- Overnight or Out-of-Town Trip for Employee and Guest
- Electronics (Television, iPod, Wireless Reading Device, etc.)
- Limousine for an Evening

THE FRIEDMAN GROUP
Retail Consulting & Training

The following programs have been designed to complement this book and enhance the professionalism of your staff and the productivity of your stores.

RETAIL SALES AND MANAGEMENT

Books, Audio, and Video Training Programs

Gold-Star Selling: *The World's #1 Retail Sales Training Course*. Videotaped before a live theater audience, this updated program captures the passion and spirit of Harry J. Friedman, retail's most sought-after consultant and trainer, as he shares his newest discoveries for making your sales staff more successful. Incorporated into the program are role-plays and interviews with shoppers and salespeople in retail stores that give your staff a new perspective on how customers want and expect to be treated. Your staff will learn how to assess customers' shopping profile and engage them in conversations that result in more sales; how the Quick Tour establishes value in shopping at your store and differentiates you from the competition—including those on the Internet; why people buy, and how to match your merchandise to their desires and routinely add on to the sale; and how to handle customer concerns and comfortably close the sale—today! Plus, they'll learn the long-lost art of customer appreciation, and how to build loyal customers for life. *Deluxe album with 4 DVDs, 5 participant's workbooks, 5 participant's checksheets, 1 coach/leader's guide, and 5 pocket reference guides. Available in General Retail, Home Furnishings, Jewelry, and Apparel/Footwear versions.*

No Thanks, I'm Just Looking: If you read only one book this year, this should be it! No one else can show you how to turn "I'm just looking" shoppers into devoted, lifelong customers like Harry J. Friedman can. You'll enjoy reading Harry's personal collection of proven selling techniques for today's retail sales floor, which will save you hours of trial-and-error experience. Included are all the tips and humorous anecdotes that have made him retail's most sought-after consultant, and made this retail's bestselling book. *240 pages of captivating reading in hardcover format.*

Retail Management Training Camp: Live recording of international retail authority Harry J. Friedman presenting retail's #1 sales management seminar. Learn how to motivate your staff and bring a passion for selling to your sales floor; how to set individual and store sales goals and see that they're met; how objectively holding your salespeople accountable for their sales will increase the quantity and quality of their sales; how to create a culture of great customer service, and more. *16 CDs plus 263-page manual with ready-to-use forms, checklists, and reference material.*

Multiple Store Supervision Course: Retail's only multi-store management seminar comes right to you in this compact, four-hour live recording for busy executives. Harry J. Friedman offers up proven techniques for effectively managing multiple stores and increasing productivity. Find out how to go from continually putting out daily fires to eliminating noncompliance and building better store managers. Discover why some stores lag behind the rest, and how to bring them quickly up to speed. Learn how often to visit your stores, what to do when you're there, and how to set up a "model" store that becomes the standard for all stores to follow. *Complete training program includes 5 CDs, plus 253-page manual.*

Retail Employee Development Course: How to recruit, hire, train, and retain top-producing retail employees. Harry J. Friedman tells you how to go from "frantically searching" to "selectively choosing" the best person for the job, and how to pinpoint the kind of salesperson that you should be hiring for your store. Learn how to build a training "system" instead of randomly training people, and discover what causes employees to stay and contribute to your success. *Comprehensive 258-page course manual.*

Retail Policies Manual: The first easy-to-customize, retail-specific store policies manual. Sample policies researched to be the most commonly used in retail today, along with points to consider in establishing the right policies for your store, are provided in this user-friendly manual. *Deluxe three-ring binder, plus sample manual on CD in Microsoft Word format that makes it simple to create and update your own policies manual.*

RETAIL SEMINARS

Professional Retail Management Course: *Want a staff obsessed with serving your customers and continually increasing sales?* Bring your management team to the completely updated, most on-target store management course in the world. Attended by retailers representing well over 50,000 stores, this seminar will show you how to manage, motivate, and train your retail staff to quickly generate more sales. Discover how you can turn your sales staff's "helpfulness" into High-Performance Selling; how to accurately and objectively set sales goals; the new sales metrics and how they impact sales; how to go from a "have-to" to "want-to" store culture; the right way to handle variation and deviation from best practices; how to master the most critical and often-overlooked steps of sales-floor management; redefined coaching techniques that improve everyone's sales performance; and how establishing esprit de corps results in better customer service and higher sales. *Three-day seminar includes comprehensive 263-page manual with ready-to-use forms, checklists, and reference material. Call for seminar dates.*

Multiple Store Supervision Course: *How to Build a Highly Accountable, High-Performance Retail Chain.* The first seminar that gives owners, area supervisors, and district managers a system for running multiple locations and getting everyone producing at higher levels. You'll learn how hitting your sales goals as a district or company is reliant on building stores individually; why setting initial performance baselines for each store is crucial; how to project sales goals and notice trends; how to develop strategic and practical plans for your stores; the importance of creating a "model store"; how to effectively staff your stores and stop settling for "average" employees; how to eliminate noncompliance; and how to go from district cop to district leader. *Three-day seminar includes comprehensive 253-page manual with ready-to-use forms, checklists, and reference material. Call for dates.*

Sales Masters Course: *Like Getting a Master's Degree in Retail Selling!* An in-depth look at the newest and most successful sales techniques in retail, developed by retail's master salesman, Harry J. Friedman. Discover how the high-performance professional prepares to sell; why the way you open the sale can mean success or failure; how a company history and quick tour can set you apart from the competition; must-ask probing questions that cause shoppers to open up and give you extra information that helps close the sale; Product Theater: the fine art of presenting and demonstrating merchandise with eloquence and emotion that results in "I'll take it!"; how adding on and selling groups of merchandise as single units can help you close more sales and build more profit; the fine art of closing the sale, and why intent is more important than technique; why properly cementing the sale results in fewer returns and more repeat business; and the long-lost art of customer appreciation and building loyal, lifelong customers. *Three-day course with an optional fourth-day certification. Call for seminar dates.*

IN-HOUSE TRAINING AND SPEAKERS

Bring Our Seminars to Your Location: The Friedman Group can deliver all or part of the above seminars, as well as training on other retail topics, in cost-effective, in-house programs that can be designed to fit your schedule. Programs can vary in length from one hour to several days.

Professional Speakers: *"The chicken was dry, but the speaker was sensational!"* Count on our dynamic speakers to make your next event one that is long remembered. Every one of our speakers is also a trainer, and well versed at implementing the Friedman Sales and Management System in the real world. No boring speeches that don't relate—just information-packed presentations that motivate and educate.

ELEARNING, PROJECT GOLD STAR, CONSULTING, AND CUSTOMIZED TRAINING

Elearning: The Friedman Group offers elearning, virtual classroom and single subject on-demand learning programs for a wide variety of retail topics. We can incorporate your existing product knowledge, sales, customer service, or management training, along with policy and procedure manuals—or create them for you, along with testing, certification and many other options. All of this is now available at breakthrough pricing that makes virtual learning affordable for small to midsize retailers, as well as global icons. Please call for more information.

Project Gold Star™: *The High-Performance Retail Sales and Management Implementation Program.* At the pinnacle of all Friedman training programs is Project Gold Star—a formula for developing a truly sales-driven, high-performance retail organization. This unique public forum for small groups of owners and senior managers consists of monthly two-day meetings for four months. It provides an organizational framework for streamlining store operations, developing your staff, and maximizing store performance. Key to this program is the personalized attention and access to our consultants, who will help with implementation questions and challenges you may face along the way. In just four months you'll learn to implement the full spectrum of Friedman Retail Sales and Management Systems, including training programs, performance standards, and accountability systems. It's the fastest way to boom your business. *Call for upcoming dates. This program can also be delivered privately, just for your stores.*

Consulting Services: As retail's most sought-after consulting and training organization, we offer strategic and tactical planning solutions for achieving your goals, as well as being a full-service training and implementation provider. From Business Improvement Audits to comprehensive sales, customer service, management, and operations systems, we provide organizational structure, benchmarking, and metrics for the full range of retail positions, utilizing the most widely implemented retail training methodologies in the world. Find out why retailers of all sizes and industries have made us their consulting and training resource.

Customized Training Programs: The Friedman Group provides customized training programs in the areas of sales, customer service, store management, operations, and product knowledge, as well as the development of customized policies and procedures manuals. Using our expert trainers, in-house writing staff, and video production facility, we can create and help implement the perfect training tools for your company—in a very cost-effective manner. Put your thumbprint on your training. Call to learn how we can provide a perfect solution for your needs.

THE FRIEDMAN GROUP
Retail Consulting & Training

For more information, **call 800-351-8040** or 310-590-1248
E-mail: info@TheFriedmanGroup.com • **Website:** www.TheFriedmanGroup.com
5759 Uplander Way, Culver City, CA 90230, USA

United States • Mexico • Central America • Colombia • Ecuador • Argentina • Chile • Brazil • New Zealand • Australia • South Africa • India